For Christin
I hope
Wandering

Eph 2:10

lots of love Shirley

Apples of Gold

Shirley Steele

Apologia

All quotations from the Bible are from
the Revised Standard Version
unless otherwise indicated.

ISBN 978 1 901566 13 0

Apologia Publications
P.O.Box 3005
Eastbourne
East Sussex
BN21 9BS
UK

Printed and bound in Great Britain by
CPI Antony Rowe, Chippenham and Eastbourne

My thanks

To David who has somehow made his voice tell the
computer what I wanted to say.
He is my Christopher Robin.

To Bert for encouraging me that I did have
something to say and for making
this book a reality.

To Andy and Debbie, whose kitchen was my haven to
write in, and for
'Shirley's Snack Box'- my sustenance.

My thanks also to all those lovely people who have
made up the patchwork of my life.

A word fitly spoken

is like

apples of gold

in a

setting of silver.

Proverbs 25:11

Contents

Introduction

How often one hears someone say, "I wish I'd asked my mother about this and that while she was alive." Or "Who taught you that?" and they answer, "It's the way my mother did it."

I don't have children to pass on helpful hints to or to share the many experiences that life has brought my way. But I do have many proxy children who might like to hear, rejoice about, or learn from my 80 years of adventure, more than half of which has been walking with a heavenly Father whom I discovered loves me, warts and all.

My earthly father had an apple farm. So apples have been prominent in my life. When I came across this proverb about apples of gold in a setting of silver, it seemed an appropriate title for what I have managed to gather together. I hope you'll enjoy it, laugh a lot, and perhaps find 'a word fitly spoken'.

Shirley

My first home in Kenya

I was born by Caesarean section on my grand-mother's kitchen table in August 1927. So neither my spelling nor lack of it, nor any of my other idiosyncrasies can be put down to brain damage at birth.

After the First World War, with much unemployment in England, my father joined the Beedock scheme, sending 50% A1 officers and 50% disabled officers to grow flax in the rich soil of Kericho in Kenya. This was to produce linen to cover aeroplane wings. Soon aluminium replaced linen and the bottom dropped out of the flax market.

My mother visited a cousin on the same scheme and so met my father. They were married in England and returned to Kenya to start growing tea and coffee instead of flax. The company of Brook Bond was born. The first five years of my life were largely in Kenya. I have just a few recollections of life there - bed legs standing in bowls of water to prevent the ants crawling up - red flannel pieces fixed to the back of our topees, which was supposed to prevent us getting sunstroke - and a walk we called "the ditchy walk" because it was bisected by deep ditches. I cannot recall what they were for. I was christened in Nairobi Cathedral but I don't know at what age.

Shirley and her brother Chris. aged 6 & 5

School days in Kent

Kenya in those days was a lonely place for women, and by the time I was five years old it had proved too much for my mother, so the family returned to England. My father re-trained in English farming and particularly in growing apples in Kent. So life for us small people was full of the excitement of wearing dungarees and Wellington boots and playing in small muddy streams with our favourite dog Gellert. He was a Border Collie and the joy of our lives, until he was led astray by a strange black Labrador into an addiction for killing chickens. As there was no cure, he had to go, much to our sorrow.

School days loomed ahead, first nursery school at "Tom Tiddlers" where I remember vividly being an oyster that was eaten by a walrus. I had to slide out of my shell and disappear under a curtain. And then I remember being a weasel in "Toad of Toad Hall" in a costume with a long tail, ably made by my grandmother's sewing lady. After that two small people boarded a train each day in Paddock Wood to start the long haul of education at a pre-prep school in Tonbridge.

Wartime

I was 12 years old when the Second World War started on 3rd September 1939. I remember standing in the driveway of our house in Brenchley and hearing my parents listening to a message from the King on the wireless. Hitler had been given an ultimatum to stop hostilities in Poland by 11am, but had not responded. I remember the King's solemn words, "We must therefore conclude that we are at war with Germany." I had no idea of course what that meant, but my father, who had been in the First World War as an 18-year-old, collecting rifles left on the battlefields of France, knew only too well. He soon joined up, but was later invalided out with a nervous breakdown, brought on by the frustration of the inefficiency around him. To begin with, the war didn't affect us very much, living in the Kent countryside as we did.

Later rationing was started and food was limited, but we were not starving. Coupons had to be saved to buy a joint of meat, which was a great treat. I remember when our Spaniel somehow found the joint and went off down the garden with it. The chase was on and the joint rescued, washed and cooked, and we live to tell the tale. There was no way that joint could have been thrown away.

The doodlebugs did affect us in the country, because we were on their direct flight path to London. They were pilot-less bombs with wings and a jet engine, programmed to cut out over London where they would descend and explode. In the country they could affect us in two ways: 1. The engines could cut out early and you never knew if they would, and 2. British fighters would try to tip their wings to bring them down before they got to London. I vividly remember hearing one flying overhead and lying flat on the pathway until the danger passed.

In those days we all slept on mattresses close to chimney-breasts downstairs, as being the safest place in the house. Petrol was rationed, so as children we travelled great distances on bicycles. I remember cycling 12 miles with my brother, to take part in a children's tennis tournament, only to be knocked out in the first round because we were so exhausted.

Evacuation – school burnt down

Next for me came boarding school, first at Winceby House, Bexhill and then in several different locations as the war loomed nearer, and we were evacuated away from the south coast. First the school moved to Herefordshire but an aerodrome appeared next door, so we moved to Wales. There a measles epidemic necessitated dormitories being turned into sick rooms and fires being lit in the bedroom grates of this beautiful Elizabethan house. Somehow sparks caught the old beams beneath the grates or in the chimneys, and a strong wind fanned them into flames, burning down the school.

We were sent off to play hockey, while the staff did what they could to save the accounts and other papers. That night we were housed in cottages roundabout and the next day sent home in what we stood up in, which in my case was my guide uniform. Clothes were rationed with coupons, so I wore some of my mother's clothes for many months before we had saved up enough coupons to replace my school uniform.

School memories

Scripture lessons, or 'Divinity', as it was called in those days, came from studying the Bible, and when you reached a certain age you were asked if you would like to be confirmed into the Church of England. We had a very fine headmistress who was a Christian. I believed in God, so I opted to join the confirmation class. It was not very instructive and was rudely interrupted by the school burning down. So when we were eventually re-housed in Berkshire and I was confirmed, I had little idea of what it actually meant, though I do remember heat slowly spreading from my toes to the top of my head when the Bishop put his hands on my head. You would expect it (if you expected anything at all) to be the other way round, from head to toe!

Other school memories include: captaining the hockey team as right back, unheard of - getting my cricket colours by catching out the captain of the local village cricket team - putting on my first pair of silk stockings - our French Mademoiselle throwing my home work down the passage and rewarding me with Ds and Rs. No doubt she was surprised when I got a credit in school certificate, as indeed I was.

Whatever French I did learn then, sometimes comes in handy and I surprise myself with what I find myself recalling, which seems to be understood and has helped in many different situations: in garages in France when our car has broken down, at a wedding in Germany when a German boy married a French girl and their common language was English, but her parents knew no German or English and so could talk to no one except themselves. My little French saved the day.

Once in Russia our small team were hosted by a headmistress who spoke no English and we knew no Russian, but she had lived in French Morocco with her husband. My limited French again prevented disaster and bridged the gap between our host and her guests.

Australian airmen on leave

The war brought many Australians to England who joined the British airmen in bomber command to help win the war in the air over Germany. My parents, through the British Council, offered hospitality to some of these men for weekends or for longer leave in the country. I remember particularly four who used to come to our home often. One had his 21st birthday with us. They all found refreshment and an interlude from the stress and strain of their task.

I remember going to Brighton in the rain with one of them, Lloyd Geiger. As we walked along the front a seagull bombed my head and Lloyd with the greatest chivalry wiped the mess out of my hair with his clean white handkerchief and threw it into the sea. My mother for many years used to write to these boys and their families, but we eventually lost touch with them. I knew Lloyd had married and we had received a picture of his wedding.

Fifty years later David and I were visiting relations in Perth Australia and I remembered that Lloyd came from Perth. I also knew he had been very ill at one time, and there was the possibility that he had died. Mentioning this to David's relatives, they encouraged me to look up 'Geiger' in the telephone book and see if I could find out anything about him. I remember it was our last evening in Perth and I took the telephone directory into another room. I found three 'Geiger's. The first one, a lady, had married into that family but was unaware of any others.

I dialled the second one. I said, "I'm from England. It's a very long shot, but I wonder if you have had a Lloyd Geiger in your family?" "Yes," she said, "He is my husband and he's standing right beside me and I know who you are, you are the English girl with the long legs." Lloyd had been ill but had recovered and they had moved away from Perth. Later they had moved back again and here they were encouraging us to come round to coffee immediately.

Lloyd whom I'd last seen when he was 23 was now 73. I had been 17 and was now 67. We wouldn't have recognized each other in the street but there we were having coffee together all these years later.

During the course of conversation I asked him if he remembered the trip to Brighton and the seagull bombing me. "Yes" he said, "And I wiped it away with my handkerchief and threw it into the sea." I was touched that his wife, who had never met me, should remember about us and be so interested to meet us.

Going out into the world

When I left school my Bible went on the shelf, as I understood it was for learning the stories so that I could pass exams. As far as I knew it had nothing to do with life. So I looked into the future with two major questions on my mind: had I done something that would somehow bias my life? And, how did I make decisions and know that they were right, or was life a sort of guessing game? I remember being asked "What do you want to do dear?" Well 'dear' didn't really know, and anyway it seemed to me that what I wanted to do wasn't a big enough reason for living.

So one lived and worked and did what one's friends did, but wondered what life was all about and what I was supposed to be doing? There were decisions to be made around every corner. Where did I work? Where did I live? And the biggest in my mind, how did one know who one should marry? What had happened to the failed, or poor, or mediocre marriages that one saw around? I didn't want my own marriage to be like those. I wanted to be some use in the world, but until I really knew where I was going myself, how on earth could I help anyone else? I worried and with worry came weariness, and I seemed to catch every cold and 'flu that there was the catch.

Fascinated at first by my grandmother's sewing lady, and then at school greatly helped by a dear matron who took an interest in my making things out of practically nothing, I left school and started dress designing at a Russian school in Earls Court, London, called Katinka. I graduated from pupil to teacher, and learnt much in the five years that I stayed there.

Good news from a friend

At school I had a sweet friend who seemed to me very superficial. I thought, very arrogantly, that if only she believed in God there would be something to her. I lost touch with her for several years but then she found me again, came to London and took me out to lunch. I looked across the table at her and found her eyes now full of peace looking back at me. This was something new. She told me she had become a Christian. I couldn't understand what she was saying. Surely we were both Christians already? She was working at a Christian conference centre and suggested that I might like to come down for a week's holiday. I thought 'anything to get out of the rat race and my round of worries'. I found a free week in July 1954 and made my way to Lee Abbey, a beautiful holiday conference centre in North Devon.

I had never met such fun loving people, who had such a sense of purpose and direction and who seemed to have all the qualities I wished I had. As I talked with them, all their stories were different but they talked about 'knowing Jesus Christ' or 'meeting Jesus Christ'. I had never heard such an expression. To me he was someone who had done something a long time ago that I didn't understand, a remote figure who I never would have thought had anything to do with life today, let alone mine.

Later that week the leader was giving a talk about the Bible and he kept holding up his left hand and putting his right hand into it, saying, "If you put your hand into the hand of Jesus Christ, he will never let you go." He seemed to be talking about Jesus as if he was alive, and all around me the people I was meeting were living as if he was alive. I suddenly thought, 'If he is alive, perhaps he's the friend I need, who knows about my life.' As I sat in that big armchair in a room full of 150 people, I spoke in my thoughts to him and said, "I really don't know what I have done with you before, but if you can do anything with my life you have it lock, stock and barrel. I'm sick of trying to run it." I didn't know what to expect.

I didn't really expect anything, but in a couple of days I had the most marvellous peace that I have ever experienced. I figured that it must be something to do with what I said in that big armchair and that if he could give me this peace he must have a purpose for me and I could quit worrying and find out what it was.

A new life

I returned to London and took down my Bible from the shelf. I dusted the mould out of the covers and started reading the New Testament. It became a new book and was talking about the experience that I was having. I was directed to a small lunch hour group studying the Bible. There we learnt what the Bible was and how to read it, and how to pray to God and begin to know him. I had been such a worrier and cautious person, afraid of making decisions, and suddenly I found myself with a totally new audacity.

Immediately on returning from Lee Abbey I heard of a friend's friend who was in a mess. She was malnourished, supposed to be marrying in three weeks and didn't know what she should do. I found myself asking for her telephone number and ringing her up, and asking to see her.

That week I made my way to Swiss Cottage to supper with her and her mother. All I could say was, "Last week I was a mess, now I am different, why not go to Lee Abbey, and perhaps you'll find the answer there too." With only three weeks to her wedding she planned to go there. I shall never forget the look of hope in her eyes as she saw me on to the bus. She went to Lee Abbey and also found Jesus Christ as I had done, and then went to her wedding completely sure she was doing the right thing and absolutely radiant.

I had always wanted to help people and now I saw that I didn't have to have the answers to people's problems, but Jesus Christ did, and I just had to get them in touch. To begin with all I could do was send them down to Lee Abbey, until I began to learn that I could help people to find Jesus myself.

Now my life was looking and feeling very different. It was like being picked up and turned 180° round in the opposite direction. I had a new confidence and a new spring in my step. I remember my first skiing holiday after that. Suddenly I was up with the others, instead of struggling with tiredness and always behind. It was quite a shock for my family and friends.

A new confidence

My family were quite worried that I had got a sort of religious mania and would never get married. Certainly the big question of marriage I felt I could leave in God's hands instead of struggling with all the emotional ups and downs of meeting people and wondering if this was Mr Right or not, and having no criteria by which to make such large decisions. With a new confidence in living and a new adventurous spirit and a new understanding of God's love and purpose, I found myself more prepared to take risks.

One such risk was when I visited some older friends for tea. They had a Finnish au pair girl whom they were in despair about, as she seemed to be very depressed and was crying all the time. Thinking she lacked young company, I offered to take her up to my flat in London for a week. In those days I was working on my own from my rented flat. I particularly enjoyed designing wedding dresses.

I had hardly got her there when I realised she was having a full nervous breakdown. The next day, not knowing what to do, I went downstairs to the communal telephone and there found a letter from the older couple with the name and number of the Finnish social worker in London. So I picked up the phone and asked her to come round. Returning upstairs, I found the girl reading my Bible and much calmer.

When the social worker arrived I told her that I was a Christian and what had happened. After she had made arrangements for the girl to go to a hostel, and just as she was leaving she said, "No one in London has ever said to me I am a Christian, come to my party on Monday."

Being more audacious these days I found my way to Swiss Cottage to her party. And so began a series of events that led first me, and then both David and me, going to Finland together many times, him leading courses for pastors and others on several occasions. And since then, both of us giving training in 18 cities in Russia and 2 in Ukraine after the collapse of the Soviet Union. Large ships turn on very small rudders. Who would have known, when I made a random decision to have tea with older friends that it would lead to such adventures in the future.

Following the social worker's party, we had to find a way for the Finnish girl to be taken back to Finland. There was a rail strike at the time but I managed to borrow a car from my parents. Someone had volunteered to accompany her on the plane if we could get her to the airport. I knew my way to St John's Wood and I knew my way to the social worker's flat from Swiss Cottage, but I didn't know the bit in between. I was also learning that God likes us to ask for help, so I thought this was a good opportunity to ask. I got to St John's Wood, stopped the car and said, "Lord now what shall I do?" I looked up and straight ahead of me was a large yellow notice that said "Diversion to Swiss Cottage". A much loved English archbishop, William Temple, coined the phrase, "When I pray coincidences happen, when I don't they don't". This was one of those times.

Adventures in the Arctic

Another outcome of that original party was a tea party with her and a friend of hers that I had also met at the first party. In the middle of the tea party Patty, the Finnish social worker, looked at me and said, "Why don't you go to Finland in July with Nalle when she is running a youth camp in Lapland?" And Nalle turned round and said, "Yes, why don't you." I was taken aback. I hardly knew where Finland was. I thought they must have been talking about it before I arrived, so not wanting to be rude, I said I would think about it. As I thought about it I began to think, Why not? Plans began to take shape and I soon found myself getting on a Russian ship for a four-day voyage through the Kiel Canal and the Baltic Sea to Helsinki. I didn't dare to tell my parents I was going to Finland on a Russian ship so I was horrified when my father said he would come and see me off.

As I travelled on my own, sometimes rather seasick, drinking Russian tea, I could hardly believe I was the same person who two years before could scarcely make a decision without a huge struggle. As we sailed into Helsinki harbour early one summer morning on a calm and beautiful day, leaning on the ship's rail I began to hear a call coming across the water. "Shirley from England? Shirley from England?" originating from behind a large pair of sunglasses on the quayside. Nalle had come to meet me. She had very little English but she asked if I was tired. On telling her I was not, she asked if I would like to accompany her to watch an athletic match between Finland and Hungry where we spent the afternoon eating ice cream and cheering on Finland. She was a sports teacher at school and at Helsinki University, and trainer of the Finnish Women's Olympic Ski Team. She later represented Finland on the Winter Olympics committee,

As we tried to communicate, we developed a language we called reindeer-ish. Words like 'sleepy' she coined as 'slippery' and so on. I'm sure that by the end of the summer other people would have had difficulty knowing what on earth we were talking about. It was a huge adventure for me to live in another country with people I didn't know, to go far above the Arctic Circle and do things that Finns love to do, get a rucksack on their back with a sleeping bag and food for a few days and a compass, and point north. We slept under the stars, round a camp fire to keep the bears away, cooked our own fish in the open on the fire we had built, and sang Finnish songs as we walked miles through the hills and the forests.

A test of my faith

Travelling the last 50 miles on a bus on rough roads, Nalle was thrown off the back seat where she was trying to sleep. She was thrown on to some milk churns. By the time we arrived at our destination she could hardly walk and was in great pain. We obviously couldn't camp with the others, but we were able to rent a small one-roomed cottage. I remember lighting the stove and putting towels round the stovepipe most of the night, and then putting them on Nalle's back to try to ease the pain. We were at Kilpisjarvi, the point where Finland, Sweden and Norway meet, where there was just one hotel that owned the small cottage we were staying in. When the group had to depart in the bus, we couldn't go with them. We tried to find a doctor but he was on holiday. The only taxi was 100 miles south and the driver was ill.

Two girls, who were walking in the area, heard that we were asking for a taxi and knocked on our door. One of them had been at school with Nalle and was a chemist. She gave us two painkilling capsules. We then heard that the taxi had rung back and the driver would come for us. The capsules coped with the six-hour drive south to Muonio, near where we had started our journey at the YWCA cottage. He took Nalle to the small hospital and me to the only small hotel. I had no Finnish language and no money, but I remember having a wonderful wash in hot water at 4 o'clock in the morning and remembering that it was my birthday.

The next day some food was put in front of me, I managed to ask for the hospital and started on the mile walk to get there. I thought, "I must take flowers." And at that moment beside me in the ditch were wild roses. Nowhere else along that road did I see anything but dried up grass. The next day I returned south to the YWCA cottage and the group. Several days later Nalle discharged herself from the hospital and also returned to the cottage, but hardly able to walk and in great pain.

Soon that first group went home and a younger group arrived, furious that their leader Nalle was unwell. Each camp had a 'body' who led the sport activities and a 'spirit' who was responsible for the spiritual side. The 'spirit' for this new and younger camp turned out to be a nursery school teacher, who had no idea how to cope with these rebellious teenagers.

One day Nalle turned to me and said, "You will do the five minute talk at tomorrow's breakfast." It was a command not a question, so I had to agree! This adventure was making me pray as I had never prayed before. So I went away with pencil and paper and sat down and said, "Lord what do I do now?" As I sat there I seemed to know exactly what to say straight from heaven, so I wrote it down and went out into the forest among the mosquitoes to learn it. When I gave it the next morning to these obstreperous girls, Nalle turned to me and said, "That was marvellous." As I felt it was nothing to do with me, but was given to me, I was inclined to agree!

Eventually these girls also had to leave, and we were on our own, not knowing how we should return south, but praying to know what we should do. First we would have to walk nearly half an hour. Nalle's back was improving, but until we actually tried this walk we wouldn't know if she could. We would then have to take a rowing boat across a small lake to where we could get a taxi, which would take us to where we could catch a local train to Rovanjemi. From there we would take the mainline overnight train south to Hyvinkaa.

We wrote for rail tickets, and eventually came the day for us to leave. Nalle managed to walk to the lake, which was as smooth as a mill pond that day, and the boat took us to the taxi, and so to the local train. Nalle's strength was ebbing away and I knew she couldn't manage the overnight bit of the journey without rest, so I started to pray for a solution. Suddenly she looked up and said that her mother would want her to stay a night in the town before taking the night train, so we had 24 hours to rest and caught the train the next evening.

After two months in Finland I eventually returned to England, having had a rather more eventful time than I could possibly have imagined, and very much the richer for it. Not only had I visited a new country and lived with people I'd never met before, but I'd seen my heavenly father answer very special prayers in what were to me very unusual circumstances.

Helpful Hints

Do it now

We had the huge privilege of living with Doug and Lila Sparks for four months in their home in Holland, in Vorburg near The Hague. As I make my bed every morning and tuck the coverlet under the pillows, I still remember that this is what Lila used to do. Other things I caught from Lila too. One was the "Do-it-now" principle. If a button needs sewing on or something needs mending, I hear Lila's voice saying, "Do it now." There is time to do those things that need doing, and it prevents the pile of "do-it-laters" mounting up until they never do get done. Thank you Leila.

Making things stick together.

"How do I get the surface I'm gluing to stay together with its counterpart until it really is stuck? We use clothes-pegs or Sellotape. Who taught me that I wonder?

Beating cream

Sometimes cream doesn't seem to want to be beaten properly or seems to take an age. Put in half to a teaspoonful of sugar before you start and you will notice the difference.

Helpful Hints

Mould

A friend was visiting and for some reason we talked about decorating. "What do you do about black patches that appear on the walls in the corners of rooms?" she said. I said, "A mixture of water and bleach applied with a toothbrush will not only clean it but also help to kill the mould spores." She had never heard that.

Sellotape to remove sticky smears

You watch those concentrated looks as supermarket sorters solemnly stamp those price tags onto glasses, china and other things? They have special guns to put them on, and they don't at the time think how they are going to come off. Nor are they near when we get them home and try to get the price tags off ourselves. Most of the time the little tag comes off all right, but it's the sticky smear that it leaves behind, that becomes the problem. We try to wash it off but it doesn't want to leave. We can use spirit but some surfaces won't take spirit, especially plastic. The answer: about 2 inches of Sellotape dabbed many times on the offending remains of the label will win in the end with complete satisfaction. If necessary keep changing the Sellotape.

Sharing flats in London

Part of London life inevitably is sharing flats. In the 12 years I worked there I must have lived in 4 or 5 flats with people I knew and people I didn't, and with many different experiences that went with them. In the late 40s and 50s working life was not so pressured and there was more time for other activities. After a period of living at home and learning more about my father's apple farm, I moved back to London to a flat near Sloane Square.

When I had a space after a flatmate had got married, I was asked by the house owners if a friend of theirs could move in with me, and so arrived another Shirley. She was working for two MPs at the time, always ahead of them. We used to tease her and asked her if she'd cleaned their teeth that morning. She was also ahead of herself. So when she arrived back at the flat she would turn down the bed and put her slippers out for the night before she even sat down for a cup of tea.

We became good friends. I hadn't long been a Christian in the sense of realising that you could know Jesus Christ personally, and realising that he had made it possible to come into a relationship with God, because he'd paid the full price of all our wrongdoings by dying on the cross and paying their penalty instead of us. It wasn't long before Shirley found Jesus too and we both became members of St.Paul's, Portman Square. There she brought her competence and management skills to the Thursday Club for young people. In the course of time she met and married David Paterson, who was ex-army and the senior curate. His fellow curate, another David was his best man and I was her bridesmaid. We two also eventually married but our paths went in different directions, theirs into parish life and ours to Kenya and elsewhere, but we remained good friends over the years.

After our adventures in Lapland, Nalle asked if I could find somewhere for a colleague to live in London, who was coming to study modern dance. I knew that if she wasn't living near me I would never get to see her. There was no room in our house, so I prayed for a space and sent her my address so she could apply for a visa. By the time she arrived several months later there was a room. And when Shirley got married Pirkko moved up to share with me. In a while she, like Shirley, soon found Christ for herself.

Much later on she came back to London to do a 3-month Agape training course, after which she was allocated to Portugal for the rest of the year working among families in the mountains above Oporto. When she retired from teaching in Finland, she continued as a missionary in Portugal for another 15 years.

An unexpected flatmate

During this time I was still going to the small lunch hour groups for new Christians at All Souls, Langham Place. There I met Marion an 18-year-old studying at secretarial college. She was the only child of a bank manager. Her family had sent her to be confirmed in the Church of England, thinking it would make her more marriageable. There she was not only confirmed, but she was taught that it meant that she was affirming that Jesus Christ was her saviour and she was his follower. This became a reality to her.

Her new direction and enthusiasm was not what her parents expected or wanted, so now they tried to correct it. They forbad her any Christian friends and took away her Christian books, but not her Bible. She used her dinner money to pay her fare to our group and shared her story with us. Eventually, on the anniversary of her confirmation, she felt she had to confront her parents with her serious intention to follow Christ, and if they didn't respond she would leave home. I remember saying that if she had nowhere to go she could come to my flat.

A few weeks later, after a weekend away, I found an extra pair of earrings on my bedside table. Marion had arrived! She let her parents know where she was, and so she stayed with us.

Some time later, I had a call one Friday from a vicar in Streatham, called Bill, whom I had met on one of my visits to Lee Abbey. A man in his congregation had met Marion's father on a train, and he had shared his anxiety about his daughter, and the man had shared this with his vicar and mentioned that Marion was staying with me. It happened that I was the only girl whom Bill knew in London, so he called and suggested that I should take Marion down to Streatham that evening.

However I had already rung home and told my mother that I was coming home for the weekend. I had made it a rule that once I had rung my mother, I never changed plans but always did what I had said. But that tea-time my mother rang me, and said that she thought it was too foggy for me to come that night and wouldn't it be better to come in the morning instead? So I was free to take Marion to Streatham to see Bill and explain the circumstances.

Subsequently Bill met up with Marion's father, and it made all the difference. His antagonism began to decline, so Marion was able to take me to her home to meet her parents. They saw that I wasn't an irresponsible teenager, but 10 years ahead of Marion and we were able to talk sensibly.

Little by little, everything got better and Marion returned home, but into a very different climate. She could freely follow her faith. Later, both her parents also became Christians, and then moved to another part of London, becoming members of a Baptist Church there. At Marion's 21st birthday party, the Baptist minister made a speech and said what a lucky girl she had been to be brought up in a Christian home. I met Marion's father's eyes across the room, and he gave me a big wink. You would hardly believe that in Britain at that time someone becoming a Christian could cause such a controversy, but we have met several others. My own parents thought I had got religious mania. And we knew one young man whose wealthy parents sent him on a cruise to get over it. It can be hard to cope with.

Vengeance

I remember one instance of God using his Word to guide me was when I was sharing a flat with a friend in Putney. I arrived home one day, opened the front door and called out "Hello." No response. So I concluded she wasn't at home. However when I went into the sitting room, there she was. When I asked her if she had heard my call, "Hello," she said, "Yes, but I couldn't be bothered to answer."

A few days later I came home, opened the door, and again called out "Hello." No answer. I supposed she was feeling the same way and I thought, "Right, I won't bother to look for her now". At that moment, into my mind came the Bible verse, "Vengeance is mine, I will repay says the Lord." And I remembered it wasn't my job to pay her back for her previous attitude, but I was to leave it to the Lord. Reproved, I began to search for her in the house and I found her upstairs in her room, ill. I was glad I hadn't continued with my vengeful attitude.

Tropical Community Development

I was running my own business, mostly making wedding and bridesmaid's dresses at the time. I began to realise that people were more important than their clothes, and I was spending too much time alone making their clothes, however creative that was.

The question was what did I do? I wasn't a nurse, a secretary or a teacher. "Lord," I said, "what should I do?" One day a friend, who was going on a trip abroad and for whom I was making some things, told me about her job working for a project run by the YWCA in Tropical Community Development for wives of students coming on courses in this country. They were looking for someone to teach crafts, dressmaking and puppet making. I pricked up my ears. This sounded to be the opening I needed. I had to go before a committee of 10 or so people and I remember thinking, "Who is interviewing who?" I was so sure I had got the job. I became the third member of the teaching team and we had students coming from all over the world on short courses.

I went on a short course of puppet making, run by the Educational Puppetry Association. The idea was that puppets could be used to put over a message in fairly primitive circumstances. You could tie a string between two trees, throw a blanket over it and you had a stage. The puppets could be used to put over a message about nutrition or child care or hygiene very simply, but powerfully. The object was to give these ladies an idea of how they could gather a group of others together and get doctors or other professionals to come and speak to them. But we also gave some skills, such as puppet making, to help them put their messages across.

To make a puppet you first have to model a head in plasticine. Every group I had put in eyes, a nose and a mouth, but left out the chin, so their models looked grotesque, like witches. I would send them home to look at people on the bus as they travelled. The next morning they would return and put chins on their puppets.

I also taught them simple dressmaking and patchwork, poster making and skills to form clubs. It was my job to take them round London to Red Cross First Aid classes and out of London to visit Women's Institutes. If you have ever tried to take 10 African ladies with no sense of time round London as a group, you will know the sometimes frustrating and scary moments that I had. Putting them on the right train or bus to get them to their homes was another headache, but I was rewarded when they turned up the next morning at the centre.

As we boarded a train on a visit to the Windsor Women's Institute, I managed somehow to lose one of my shoes under the train as I got on. When we asked a porter for help, he said he thought we should wait until the train had gone. Imagining my shoe being cut to ribbons as the train chugged away and having to spend the rest of the day shoeless, I implored him for a better solution. Eventually a pole was found and my shoe was rescued and I joined 5 large African women rolling around the carriage with laughter.

Other recollections of those happy years working with this project include taking a group to the Jersey Women's Institute. Some of them had never used a European toilet and needed help to understand that you don't stand on the seat, you sit on it.

At the end of one of the courses those of us on the staff found that we had acquired nicknames. Mine was 'Miss Excellent But' coined because of my repeated instruction, "That's excellent (always encourage when teaching), but I think we'd better pull it undone and start again."

With a friend at Lee Abbey

Right from 1954, when I discovered that Jesus Christ was alive, and had risen from the dead, and that I could know him and be part of his purposes and that he was longing for everyone to know him, life has been a huge and fascinating adventure with all sorts of unexpected turns.

One such adventure was when I returned to Lee Abbey with a friend who seemed interested to know more about God and his redemptive plan. She was strong and independent. I didn't know her well and was unfamiliar with her past. Lee Abbey is a beautiful place on the north coast of Devon. There are wonderful walks along the cliffs above the sea, and also a lovely cove with a beach to bathe from.

One day the wind was boisterous and the waves high and the undercurrent strong. My friend, unfamiliar with tides and undercurrents thought it looked a challenge and that with her strengths she would be quite capable of coping with such a sea. Nothing would persuade her otherwise and in she plunged. All I could do was pray and watch, as she struggled for her life and only just managed to fight the undercurrent and get out alive, wide-eyed and rather subdued.

The evening programmes were all voluntary, but most people joined in. There may have been a talk about the Bible, or someone's experience, or a panel to answer the many questions people might have about the meaning of life. One such evening was quite challenging, and a few of us wanted to pray together as a result. My friend wouldn't join us and went to our room. The rest of us prayed and then I went to join her. I found her coming down a small staircase, and she expressed huge shock when she saw me. Whatever the battle going on inside her, it turned out she felt suicidal. She had gone to our room and written a note to her mother and was now making for the cliffs. In God's mercy I appeared at just the moment to stop her. I neither knew the battle she was coping with, nor could I have planned the time I arrived on the staircase. Only God knew these things.

On another occasion we drove along the coast road to Minehead to visit an aunt of mine for the afternoon. It was a rainy and misty day, and on our return my friend suddenly said that she wanted to walk the rest of the way home and I could leave her to do it. I was beginning to get the picture that you don't reason or plead with her, her battle was with God and I had to let her do whatever she wanted. So I opened the door and let her walk out into the mist.

However, I knew and she knew, that we were about to come to where the road ran close to the cliff edge. I also knew she was again making for the cliff and being driven to take her own life again. All I could do was sit in the car and pray, at the same time wondering what I would do if she succeeded in throwing herself over the cliff. Would I drive back to Lee Abbey and say, "I lost her over the cliff?" Would I contact her mother and tell her what had happened? I sat there in the mist with my head on the steering wheel praying. After about half an hour I heard a cry and a tiny voice asking if she could come in. Wet through and shaking, she joined me back in the car and we drove on to Lee Abbey. I was learning extraordinary lessons and wisdom from God.

As she got out of the car, she thought and I thought we were just about at the point where the road we were on joined the cliff road. In fact that junction was a mile or so before one came near to the cliff edge, so that when she reached the junction, the cliff wasn't there and her plan was thwarted. And she had to turn back to find me in the car.

At the end of that week, after the evening talk I suggested we went to the chapel to pray. My friend wouldn't come, but I went anyway. Again I was aware of a spiritual struggle in her. I became convinced I should stay in the chapel until she also came there. People came and went and the time lengthened into the end of the day. As people made their way to bed, the house became quiet. I thought of Jesus' prayer in the Garden of Gethsemane, and the disciples, instead of watching with Jesus, going to sleep. I wondered how much of the night I should wait there for my friend to come, but I kept the picture of Jesus praying in the garden in my mind and thought, if he could stay all night then so must I.

We shared a room with a Danish girl. I heard footsteps approaching, and there she was saying, "Your friend says you should come to bed." "You may not understand what is happening", I said, "but just go back and say that you couldn't make me come." There was another long wait and then more footsteps. And my friend came herself, not to me, but to submit to the Lord and to find his forgiveness and peace.

Marriage

For a girl in middle class society in England in the 1950s, there was much more emphasis on getting married than on having a career as such, though we all had some sort of employment and many of us worked in London. Computers and rapid communication were non-existent and life was far less pressured than it is today. Most of those around me worked 9-5 and so there were greater opportunities for a social life in the evenings, as well as at weekends. One was constantly meeting new people and new potential husbands, and there was always the question, how did one know whom one should marry? I found the whole scenario emotionally exhausting and upsetting.

When I found Jesus Christ and the reality that he had a purpose for me, the worry and confusion left me and I concentrated on this new amazing and fulfilling life, and the excitements around every corner. I felt I could trust him to show me about marriage too.

The more I read the Bible, the more relevant I realised it was to life. As it says in 2 Timothy 3:16, it is relevant:
1. to teach the facts about God and Jesus Christ and the Holy Spirit and their purposes for the world and the people in it;
2. to show us when we are going wrong;
3. to get us back on the right path;
4. to teach us how to live rightly.

There are general principles for right living but also there are numerous references that God will direct and guide individuals. "Thy word is a lamp to my feet." Psalm 119:105 "Trust in the Lord with all your heart, ….. and he will make straight your paths." Proverbs 3:56, "Be transformed, to prove in experience how good and acceptable and perfect God's will is." Romans 12:2 "He has prepared good works for us to walk in." Ephesians 2:10

Monday Nights and the new curate

Quite soon after asking Jesus Christ into my life I had a letter from Colin Kerr, the vicar of St Paul's, Portman Square, London. I knew his niece and she must have mentioned me to him. The letter was inviting me to a weekly evening in his house called 'Monday Nights', where young people could come and have coffee and ask questions on any subject we cared to mention. I quickly joined this group and became part of an enthusiastic bunch of young Christians exploring life from a Christian point of view. We got very excited about what we thought we could all do and poured out our ideas to the vicar, whose response was, "Wait till the new curate arrives".

When the new curate arrived I discovered he was a childhood friend, whom I hadn't seen for 10 years. He soon tactfully got us all under control and into some helpful courses and groups where we flourished. A year on, he rang to ask me something. I offered him a meal, expecting him to come and talk about the groups. We had our meal and sat down with a cup of coffee, whereupon he asked if I would share his life with him? In other words would I marry him? What a bombshell and a shock, and I burst into tears. I was enjoying the peaceful existence of no involvements, and here was this man shattering my peace.

I hadn't ever been out with him. I wasn't the slightest bit interested in a relationship with him. However he was a godly man who wasn't joking and I found myself agreeing to meet him, although I thought the very idea of marriage to him was quite impossible. He was two years younger than me, and I had always known men eight or so years older than I was. There were so many things I couldn't imagine doing with him. There were many barriers in my mind. There was so little he knew about me, so the whole idea seemed extraordinary and utterly impossible. I certainly didn't love him, so what on earth was going on?

The next day, as I was washing my hands before leaving my work, the Bible verse "We love, because he first loved us" came into my mind. We love God because we were first loved by him, a responsive love. So I saw that perhaps this potential relationship with David wasn't mad after all. If it was right, perhaps I would love because I was first loved.

But then there was the whole question that I wasn't interested, nor I could see how I ever could be? I was in a group of girls who met to study the Bible each week and our next study was in Philippians chapter 2. As we looked at this passage, verse 13 leapt out of the page for me, "It is God who works in you to will (or to want) and to do his good his pleasure." "Okay Lord" I said, "If you can work in me to want this relationship, I will know this is your purpose for me."

As we met once a week on David's day off, gradually one by one the barriers I had in my mind, making it impossible, came down and I could say to the Lord "If this is your desire for me, I can now say it's mine too.

I was very aware that if I was going to be a minister's wife, girls would come to me and say, "Can I trust God for marriage?" I needed to be able to say, "Yes you can, because I did." Now I had got to the point when I could say, "Lord I believe you've worked a miracle in me and I want to marry David, but it seems to me that your timetable is as important as your will, so please tell me when I can tell him?"

He had not asked me to marry him for many months, but that week we met and he asked me again. I found I could say nothing, and I left that evening feeling quite perplexed. I had got to the point where I wanted to marry him and yet I couldn't tell him! Was I mad? Couldn't I understand what God might want, or what? At that time I was reading through the Psalms as I travelled up to London to my work each day. The next day I had got to Psalm 39. Three times in that Psalm comes the phrase, "I was dumb and I opened not my mouth, because the Lord has done it". This was too much of a coincidence! If I was mad, that was one thing, but if God had closed my mouth so that I couldn't tell David where I was at, that was another. I was not mad and there was a purpose.

Skiing in Lapland

Meanwhile, I had been asked to return to Finland to a ski camp in Lapland, so I pursued making plans for that. By this time David's mother thought I was keeping him waiting too long. And my mother was worried about what people would think if I disappeared off to Finland for an indefinite period. She couldn't understand that our friends knew nothing about our meetings. David had felt it was either for everyone to know, if it was on, or for nobody to speculate about if it was not, so we were careful not to be seen together in public.

The week before I left for Finland I became completely convinced I could tell him. It was 14 months since he'd first asked me. We went for a picnic on Ashdown Forest. David suddenly turned to me and said, "What has the Lord been saying to you recently?" Knowing this would radically change my life, but knowing that God had guided so specifically, I said, "He just showed me I can tell you that I can marry you." I imagined that we would go back to my parents and ask them (you did that in those days), but we were both so shocked, and David had got to the point of thinking, "If Abraham had to wait 13 years to receive the promise, so might he." We didn't mention it again that day, and off I went to Finland with nobody but us two knowing anything about it. I didn't know when I would return, and David's letters had to come first on a plane to Helsinki then a train to Rovaniemi in the Arctic Circle, then a bus to Muonio and finally a reindeer sledge to the YMCA cottage, Keimio.

It was the most popular Easter camp in Finland and I'd agreed to go only very shortly before it started. I found that all my tickets were in the name of 'Rousa Toivenan' meaning 'Rose Little Hope'. Nalle had booked an extra place months before, and I had walked into it. Two months later I returned to England.

In the meantime David arranged to play golf with my father and ask him for his daughter's hand. In the event, because my father had hurt his thumb, he arranged for David to play golf with our gardener, who was the Sussex champion with a plus-two handicap. So David had to spend 3 hours on the golf course with him instead of talking with my father. However, later that day he was able to spend time with my parents and was able to ask if he might marry me.

A surprise announcement

I arrived back in Britain on the night when our young people's group met. That particular Monday the vicar was away, so they were meeting in David's mother's flat. When the Bible discussion was over, David told them that in the vicar's absence it was his privilege to announce an engagement. He went into a long story about the girl and eventually said it was me. There was a silence. You could see the news sinking in, and then the question on their faces was, "Who was the chap?" David then said he was going to ask the mythical man to put a ring on her finger. All eyes were upon him, wondering who he was going to ask to come over to me. Instead of that, David went round the group and himself put a ring on my finger and gave me a kiss. Utter silence reigned as the realisation dawned, then a roar of recognition.

When the news was out, we were greatly encouraged by a couple who, on the next Sunday morning, brought us a jam jar as a gift and said they had been praying about whether we should get married. I had known the girl and David had known the man, but they had no idea if we even knew each other beyond attending the same church. Another lady said to us, "Don't think I didn't guess." We would have been surprised if she had guessed. "Well," she said, "it wasn't that I guessed, but I just knew you should."

There are many pressures on a minister's life and family, and there are many times when one can be tempted by the enemy to doubt one's marriage. Had one done the right thing? Or had one married the right man? At those times one's feelings are utterly unreliable and one has to stand firm on the guidance of God and his sure Word.

Living in a culture of opulence and increasing discontent all around, and because there are less distinctive roles for husbands and wives to play and very high divorce rates in the world and also among Christians, it is so important to know what Christian marriage is all about. In the account of God's creation of man in Genesis, we read that God said, "It is not good that man should live alone, I will make him a helper suitable for him." God's creation of woman was for the purpose of being different but complimentary. I see my primary purpose is to be David's wife, and whatever else I may also do is to help fulfil that role.

About to be given away by her father

Where to serve a second curacy?

When we became engaged, David was finishing his first curacy in London, and there were three options for his next appointment. He was asked by Kuwait Oil to go as a chaplain to St Paul's, Kuwait. He was also asked to become Associate Minister by an Episcopal Rector in Chicago, who had just invited Jesus Christ into his life and wanted help to grow as a new Christian. A whole new world was opening up in front of him.

The third invitation was for the second time from Eric McLellan to become his curate at St Nicholas, Sevenoaks. As we planned our wedding for September, I remember clearly one day being completely sure that he would ring up and tell me we were going to Sevenoaks. This is exactly what he did. I was so pleased, as it was only 40 minutes from my parents home in Crowborough, where my mother had Parkinson's disease. So we could visit her often.

My early marriage mistakes

Even though we were two Christians marrying, and I was sure I was doing the right thing in marrying David, I went into marriage with the idea that it was a sort of glorious Christian partnership. I had married a quiet man who made decisions slowly, while I had been busy running my own life and making my own decisions. So when David didn't make a decision quickly, I did. When friends came for a meal and David didn't start the conversation quickly, then I did. When it was a question of going from A to B, I always knew the best way. After a year David had gone behind a thick wall of self defence, to protect himself from this woman who was taking over his life. I wasn't happy. And I wasn't making him happy. I was thoroughly disillusioned about Christian marriage.

For our first holiday David took me to stay with a lovely Christian couple in Holland, Doug and Leila Sparks. I looked at their marriage and thought it looked all right. One day I was in Leila's bedroom with her and she started talking about marriage and all the things that wives do wrong. I ticked them all off in my mind. I had done them all. However, she gave me a Bible study and as I studied it I saw that I had been stealing David's role as a husband and leader.

So the next time he didn't start a conversation at dinner, I counted 10 before I spoke and found he came in at about 9 and led the conversation on. I began to not always know the best way from A to B. I didn't always jump in first and make all the decisions. After three months, an eye came out from behind this thick wall, to see if it could be possibly true that I was changing. After six months a toe came out. He became so grateful that I was no longer stealing his role that love came pouring my way, which was exactly what I needed to flourish, and I didn't have the burden of being the leader, but could be fulfilled in being a 'suitable' or perfect helper.

The second purpose of marriage

In the New Testament in Ephesians 5, Christian marriage is clearly defined as being a visual-aid to the world of the relationship between Christ and his church. The man is to play the role of Christ, to love his wife as Christ loved the Church, and the wife's role is to respond to that love by obedience and fitting into his life. What a privilege to be part of that visual-aid that the world should see and be drawn to Christ. It may take a lifetime to learn my part, but I am so glad that I have begun.

Mind you there have been times when I have locked myself in the bathroom and said, "Lord I'll have to stay in here until you change my attitude." In experience I've come to find out that it is the most fulfilling role one could want. You might expect that wouldn't you, because it's what woman is created for. It means that increasingly you are not treading on each other's toes, because you are each fulfilling your different purpose in God's plan.

David's gratitude

David's gratitude in giving him the freedom to be the leader he was created to be, because I'm not trying to play his role, is expressed in increasing love for me. He also includes me in what he is seeking to be and to do. I can be a sounding board in small and bigger ways. Because he needs help to know what tie goes with what shirt, it doesn't mean he isn't a fount of wisdom on many more complicated matters. Wives, we don't do well if we don't use our husbands as a sounding board for our own wisdom. They so often come up with what we haven't thought of and which can spare us much heartache. The rewards of fulfilling this role as a wife are immense. I once talked to a friend, who said he had asked a friend of his why he had become a Christian. And his friend said, "When I saw how that couple behaved towards one another." And it was us. I can keep going on that memory for a long time.

I am rewarded by what my husband accomplishes, sometimes at great cost and effort to himself. Many are encouraged, taught, trained, counselled, renewed, and also warmed by my tea. I remember saying to David recently, "I haven't helped you much today, and he replied, "Yes you have, because you were there." I may spend an inordinate amount of time just washing up and home making, which most women's magazines would decry as second-class compared to sticking on stamps in someone else's office. But then come the times of inclusion in some important and thrilling something, or the prayerful brainstorming about a vision we might have to try to bring to pass.

There have been many visits to Russia when I have slept on uncomfortable settees, washed clothes in impossible bathrooms, and where there is a partial flood whenever you turn on the hot tap. But I have shared in the experience of meeting people who are poor as church mice but would give you their last crust, born out of suffering. Psalm 68:13 says, "The women at home divide the spoil, though they stay among the sheepfolds." (RSV) or "The women at home divided what was captured." (TEV)

Parish life for a new curate's wife

When we arrived in Sevenoaks straight after our honeymoon, I found as the curate's wife I was expected to be at all activities, the Mothers Union, the Young Wives, the Youth Fellowship, and everything else that happened. I had previously had a job and a flat to run, but now I also had a husband to care for, who needed three meals a day. We didn't have washing machines in those days, and I remember washing sheets and towels in the bath and all our clothes by hand. I asked the church warden's wife, how I was supposed to manage and she just said, "I don't know my dear, but you just have to."

My aim at that time, as I went from meeting to meeting, was to try and remember people's names and hope that I would get them right next time round several meetings later, having met at least 100 people a week in the meantime.

Fortunately we were in contact with The Navigators in London, with whom David had experienced some really practical discipleship training at their headquarters in Colorado. We heard they were running training on Saturdays in London, and David suggested I join them. When they said we would visit a block of flats near Victoria Station and tell people who Jesus Christ was and what he had done for them, we were reluctant trainees. However when we went to those flats, we discovered that people were hungry to know and that we were equipped to explain it to them. This completely changed my aim in life.

Now I could aim very much further than remembering people's names. Back in the parish at the first Mothers Union meeting I was able to tell a lady how I had found Jesus, and the difference that he had made in my life. Immediately she asked, "Could I have that faith?" I invited her to tea and explained how she could.

Another thing that made sense in a big and busy parish was to work with a small group of people. In Sevenoaks I had a weekly Bible study for four people. I remember one lady saying that it meant more to her than a lifetime of going to church. I had not been to Theological or Bible College, but had received a few tips from David and we really learnt together.

When we were about to go to Kenya I learnt how people can put you on a pedestal. When I suggested to the group that they continue to meet and lead the studies themselves, they said, "We couldn't do that, after all you have been to Theological College." It made me realise how easy it is for people to attach experience to you that you haven't had, and how important it is to share who one really is, so that they can identify with you.

Hospital experiences

The completely new life I was leading as a curate's wife, masked a new tiredness that was eventually discovered to have a more serious cause. Getting 'flu and not recovering from it caused my doctor to send me to hospital, where blood transfusions and an operation followed. I learnt about hospital life, and in particular about Sister Griffiths. She was our ward sister from Wales, and ruled with a rod of iron but with a heart of gold beneath it. So when the morning after the operation, while breakfast was being served, I heard the command, "This is for number 6 and I want her sitting up," I knew there was no escape.

During those days in the ward I was the insider and David was the visiting minister. I could tell him who everyone was and who to visit. When I was discharged Sister Griffiths gave me permission to visit her ward at any time. Sadly lack of strength didn't permit it, but I would have dearly loved to have done it.

Helpful Hints

Do you dread ironing sheets?

Your arms aren't big enough and it's always on the floor somewhere!

Wherever you do your ironing, first fold the sheet (un-ironed) twice lengthwise, smoothing as you go, and getting the edges together as neatly as you can. Then fold the other way, keeping the second fold slightly short of the top! When you take the next fold pull the underneath one up with you. The sheet is now folded as if to put it neatly away. Now take it to the ironing board and iron between the folds. Take a little extra care with the top folds. By the time your sheet comes out of the airing cupboard again it will look pristine on the bed!

Blood and wedding dresses

If you've ever made a wedding dress and pricked your finger, suddenly to your horror there is a bright red spot right in the front of the bodice! Water won't wash it away, and you dare not use water on that special material anyway. Take a long thread of white cotton or silko and chew it briefly. Then take the small cotton ball and work away at the spot. The digestive juices from your mouth will deal with the stain and leave no mark or ring on the material. This is the tip for many other situations where blood has left a mark. You can place a paper handkerchief behind the stain.

A right angled tear on material or a long tear on a sheet

It can look impossible to mend, but can be simply dealt with by using a 'herringbone stitch' that can be strong enough not to tear in that place again.

Trim off the edges slightly so that there are no floating threads and the two edges can meet neatly. Thread your fine needle with appropriate thread of the right colour. Do not use a knot to start your stitch, but rather attach it firmly at one corner of the tear. Then work your 'herringbone stitch' along the line, putting your needle under the edges so that they fit neatly together, ⅛ to ¼ inch on the material each time is enough, and stitches don't need to be closer together than that either.

Sewing on a button

Don't knot the end of your thread. Hold the button ⅛ inch away from the material as you attach it. Just before you end off, bring the needle out between the button and material, and then wind the cotton round and round under the button, making a shank. Then take the needle to the back of the material to end off. This way the button is strongly held on, and the distance between button and material allows the buttonhole to lie flat and not look pinched.

Replacing a zip

Never try to put in or replace a zip by machine. The foot of the machine will slightly push the material along, making it 'bubble'. Do it by hand, using a back stitch ¼ inch apart, with only a tiny stitch on the material side. The zip will lie nicely flat and the stitches will hardly show.

Africa calls

After almost three years as a curate in Sevenoaks, David was asked by The Navigators, an international missionary organisation that he had studied with earlier, to go to Kenya for two years to work with a team of five Kikuyu men. They had been recruited to run the Bible correspondence course for the thousands of ex Mau Mau who were in the detention camps after that evil movement had been defeated. After much prayer, David became convinced that this was the Lord's next step for us.

My mother had Parkinson's disease, and I realised that this move would be unpopular with my family. I knew that if I ever doubted David's guidance on this I would have problems. So I took some time to find my own assurance of God's guidance. There was sufficient money and help in my family to look after my mother, and my brother and his wife were in England. Married to David I felt my first loyalty was now to him.

Holland

Before leaving for Kenya, The Navigators arranged for us to have 4 months living in Holland with Doug and Leila Sparks and their family from the USA. He was their European Director. I watched this family working out biblical principles in their lives. Doug was head of the family and Leila was a very supportive and loving wife. If Doug was away then Leila was the boss. If Leila was also away she appointed a substitute boss. So everyone knew where they were, the boundaries were clear, with the result — four happy non-frustrated children. One picture I will always remember is of Karen aged 3 sitting on her potty with a toy telephone in her hand, talking to an imaginary friend and saying, "We're going on vacation for a hundred years."

As well as learning all we could from this lovely family and getting reoriented back into Navigator methods and principles, David had the mornings free to think about a subject of his choice. So he chose to think out from past experience the best way to lead small groups, particularly in relation to studying the Bible. Later in Kenya he was asked by Shell Kenya to participate in a seminar which included small group leading. This confirmed many of the principles that he had been working out on his own.

One of the great strengths of The Navigator's success and growth over the years has been their emphasis on training. One of their teaching mottos is, "Tell why, show how, get him started, keep him going, and help him to help someone else." Their vision is not just to add but to multiply, and their primary method to achieve it is one-to-one training. Part of this training has been to share their homes with potential trainees at considerable cost to themselves. In doing so, they have been prepared to expose their own lives and attitudes to those of us who had the privilege of living with them. So we not only learnt first-hand from them, but could also see biblical principles being worked out in daily life. We could catch how to follow Christ.

Funeral at sea

After Christmas in England with our families, in January 1963 we sent our luggage to Tilbury in that extremely severe winter when many roads became impassable due to thick ice. We were so fortunate that it got through to the Union Castle Line ship sailing for Kenya that we planned to join later. We had more time with our families and avoided sailing through The Bay of Biscay in mid-winter, by going by train to Genoa, Italy, and joining the ship there.

At our table there was an elderly lady and her companion. It was incredibly rough crossing the Mediterranean, and I remember lying on a chaise-long on deck next to her, and her saying something like she was glad I was there. I felt so ill I didn't say much, and later bitterly regretted not talking to her about how much God loved her, because a day or so later she died before we arrived in Port Said. David, as a minister, was asked to take her funeral at sea, and her companion left the ship at Port Said. We learnt later that she and her husband, a founder of Petters Engineering, had been very keen sailors, and she wanted to die at sea. So she spent much of her time on cruises and other sea voyages.

We met some lovely people on that ship, including a missionary doctor and his wife and their small daughter, also a Dutch couple who joined the ship at Aden and sailed with us to Mombasa. They had been hoping to drive from Cairo-to-The Cape but were forced to bypass Sudan because of the dangers there at that time. David, having been an engineer, had good times of Bible study on deck with some of the ship's engineer officers when they were off duty.

Adventures in Kenya

By the time we arrived at Mombasa we were re-freshed after the rigours of packing and saying 'goodbyes'. We were ready to meet what Kenya had in store for us. We had a lovely day in Mombasa with Chris and Jane Hindley before boarding the over-night train to Nairobi. There we stayed with Robert and Sarah Howarth for about 2 months, while we looked for a suitable home before they left to work in England. David and Robert had spent 11 days crossing The Atlantic together in 1955, and then the next 9 months or so at The Navigator headquarters in Colorado Springs.

After a couple of months we found an eighth floor flat at the top of Church House in the centre of Nairobi. This proved ideal, since it was at the meeting point of the European, African and Asian areas of the city, and therefore accessible to all ethnic groups. It was also ideal for security. When we travelled away from Nairobi, we could shut the door and know the flat was secure. I remember the first time we went out at night, the bundle of rags by the main door at the bottom of the lift moved, making us jump. This turned out to be Sospeter, a lovely Christian night-watchman from Luo country. Our daily contact with him was very sweet, together with his nightly greeting, "Habare Nairobi?" As we travelled around the country in our small Morris Minor van meeting the team and working with them, we learnt so much. Only Arthur was working in the office in Nairobi.

It's not wrong, it's different.

Before we left for Kenya I asked Leila Sparks, who had gone with her husband Doug to the Philippines early in their marriage, what she would say to a new wife embarking on a 2-year assignment to Kenya. "It's not wrong, it's different," she said. Easy to remember, that piece of advice has stood me in good stead on many occasions. On arrival in Kenya I somehow expected the African culture to be different but I expected the European culture to be more like my own. So when I confronted small differences in table manners for instance, the advice, "It's not wrong, it's different," dealt with my judgemental spirit and put it in its place. Through the years in many circumstances and on many occasions it has saved the day by controlling my attitude.

I must have passed this advice on to many people because recently, visiting friends we hadn't seen for 35 years, the husband said that someone had passed it on to him many years ago mentioning they had heard it from me and been helped by it as he himself had also.

Perhaps this is a small example of what Paul meant when he wrote to Timothy in 2 Timothy 2:2 "What you have heard from me among many witnesses, the same entrust to faithful men who will be able to teach others also." Let's keep passing on good things to others.

Rehoboam and Elizabeth

Rehoboam Mwiri and his wife Elizabeth lived with their two children high above The Rift Valley. I remember one visit to them when we stayed overnight. Their friends were invited in to share a meal. Someone brought chickens and others brought vegetables. There was a fork each and one knife to pass round, and we talked until the smoke from the fire gradually got lower and lower in the room until it got into our eyes and the friends departed.

Rehoboam and Elizabeth gave us their single bed and they slept on a pile of banana leaves in their kitchen. They brought a jug, a bowl of water and a towel to the living room so we could wash our hands and faces and clean our teeth while everyone watched. Sometimes little hands crept up the back of our necks to feel our European type hair. The loo was at the bottom of the garden, just a hut with a hole in the ground and some boards across the gap.

We had shared with joy in their living conditions and they came to Nairobi to share in ours. I remember one week-end when they had asked to bring friends. They took them down the passage to the bathroom to show them how the WC worked. There were guffaws of laughter as they had never seen anything so funny. I also remember a meal in our home with Rehoboam and others when I had made a cherry pie. It was quite natural for him to spit the cherry stones out all over the carpet and the parquet floor. On his mud floor at home it was easy for Elizabeth to sweep them up in the morning, but I had to hold my hair on metaphorically and say nothing as the stones clattered and bounced around the room.

How we loved Rehoboam and Elizabeth. I remember thinking, that if anything ever happened to David, it would be to Rehoboam that I would turn. Elizabeth didn't have much English, but we could use the Bible as a phrase book and talk together with its help. Rehoboam had some sort of sleepy sickness and quite often would completely nod off during a meeting. He always wore a knitted hat that looked more like a tea cosy.

Bartholomew and Lois

Bartholomew and Lois had each been the only Christian in their family, and their prayers were that God would somehow arrange for them to marry a Christian. Their families thought them worthless, because they wouldn't brew or drink the strong homemade alcohol called 'Pombe'. Not knowing what to do with these worthless children, their parents eventually decided to marry them off to each other. Bartholomew's and Lois's prayers were wonderfully answered.

They had six children and a small farm at Githunguri. We often visited them there and Lois would bake cakes and make tea, and they would tell us stories of the Mau Mau times and the danger that Christians had been in. On one visit, a neighbour called in to meet us. He later disappeared, only to return a short while later with a live chicken which he wanted to give to us. David quietly asked Bartholomew how many chickens he had. The answer was six. And Bartholomew told us we must receive it. It was a huge gift.

The chicken had to be alive as it would quickly deteriorate in the heat if killed, and wouldn't be fit for anyone to eat. That evening we were giving Peter, Bartholomew's eldest son a ride back to Nairobi, so we asked him what we should do with this live chicken. He replied, "Put a string round its neck and tie it to one of the bath taps." Fortunately we remembered that we would be passing the home of Cyrus, so we asked him if he would look after the chicken. After that, every time he came into Nairobi he would bring eggs laid by this chicken, until we said that as he provided the food for the chicken, he should keep the eggs.

One weekend we had a small conference for the wives of our team. Josiah, Lois' youngest son was four at the time, so we asked her who was looking after him. Apparently he was looking after their cow all day, which meant that the cow was looking after him. Margaret, a 10-year-old sister who was at school, would bring him his lunch and return to look after him at the end of the day.

Africans at that time tended to think that the 'Wazungu', as whites were called, knew all the answers to everything. So Lois was surprised when I asked her how she taught her children to pray. At first she thought it was a sort of test; did she know the right answer? Eventually she said, "When he's a baby, I thank God for him. But when he's old enough to do it for himself, he thanks God." What a non-question I had asked.

Evans and Esther

Evans had been an ardent Mau Mau as a teenager, so when he found Christ as his saviour he was equally ardent in his new found faith and the reality of his new relationship with the Lord. He wanted to tell others of this wonderful truth and encourage them to walk with God. He lived north of Nairobi helping a Christian minister. I remember we arrived one day and his cow had just eaten his shirt which was hanging on the line to dry. Our little Morris Minor van bumping across the dusty roads heralded our arrival and visitors from the huts around would come to visit Evans and these strangers. We might have had a hut full of neighbours all the time while we were there, but Evans would welcome them and let them stay 5 or 10 minutes, and then say, "Now I must release you, you have things to do", and they would have to get up and leave.

When Evans was about to move to a new place of ministry at Mwea, near Mt.Kenya, he prayed that he would be able to help one man to know Christ in each of the five villages around. And wonderfully a man in each village came to know Jesus quite soon. It was quite easy in the dry season to help Peterson Degwa, who lived on the other side of the river, because they would meet under a tree and shares spiritual truths and their applications from what they had been studying in the Bible. But during the rainy season, with no bridges for miles either way and with the river roaring past, they would have to shout to each other across the torrent.

Cyrus and Anna

Like Evans, Cyrus had been a Mau Mau teenager. At the Kenyan Navigators 50 year celebrations in 2006, Cyrus was able to tell of his conversion and of the beginnings of the work in the late 50s and 60s, and of the Lord's faithfulness to his family since then. Soon after Kenya's independence in 1964 he was employed by Shell. Later he and his wife started a clothing business.

Their church was very close to a market and, like many other Kikuyu churches, had loudspeakers on the roof, so that everyone in the market place could hear what was going on inside the church and hopefully be encouraged to come in and hear more. Forty years on Cyrus is still a faithful elder of his church and, like Evans, is putting Navigator principles into practice.

Arthur and Philisia

Arthur was the remaining member of the team working in the office when we arrived in Nairobi, so we saw a lot of him and enjoyed him and his wife Philisia living nearby. They had three lovely children.

No money to pay the team

One Friday, we realised we had no money to pay the team's monthly wages to support them and their 27 dependents. We had no one to go to, as by that time we were the only Europeans on the Navigator staff in Kenya. But we could pray and ask God for his help.

On the Monday morning a cheque arrived in the post for the exact amount that we needed, from someone who had never given to the work before and who never gave again. God met our needs perfectly.

Team re-employment

David felt strongly that, as Kenya was about to become independent, it was important that the team members became indigenously employed in Kenya rather than being supported by a student ministry in the USA. The Navigator leadership agreed. At independence all foreign missionaries could have been turned out of Kenya, and we didn't want to see these men and their families without any income. We also felt they would be more useful as 'inside men' sharing their faith with the people where they worked.

Rehoboam became a radio pastor with the Africa Inland Mission at Kijabi. Listeners sometimes walked 3 or 4 days from Tanzania to ask him questions and get further wisdom from him.

Bartholomew became an evangelist on 'death row' in Nairobi prison and was able to help many find their Saviour.

About that time the government ordered all businesses to take on 10% extra staff. In the event the remaining members of the team were taken on by Shell Kenya, Arthur and Cyrus to do office work, and Evans to work in the Nairobi distribution depot.

Evans was concerned about how to get to know his fifty fellow workers, so he and his wife, Esther, and we prayed about this. He and his wife came up with the idea that, if she made double the number of sandwiches that he would eat, he would be able to invite one of his colleagues to have lunch with him and talk with him about Christianity. This was extremely fruitful, several coming to know Jesus.

Cultural differences

In Kenya we learnt first hand about differences of colour, customs and culture and the need to understand them to forestall misunderstandings. By close contact with our team of five and all their families, we learnt that whatever differences there are in people, their hopes and joys, and sorrows are much the same and that the Bible has the answers and love is the way. These were valuable lessons to learn as we have subsequently lived among many different groups in the world, and it has given us confidence to easily meet and mix with many different people groups.

One day we met a young Kikuyu man who was looking for a job and asked to see us at 9am one morning. He appeared four hours late. We were not impressed. When we asked why he was late, he replied, "It was raining." We were even less impressed. Talking this over later with one of our team, we learnt that actually he had done us a good turn by not coming while it was raining. Apparently in Kikuyu custom, if someone arrives, having got very wet, you are obliged to give him fresh clothes to replace his wet ones. How important it is to understand the culture of those whom we go to live amongst. It can be so different from one's own.

Beware of imagining other's thoughts

Frances and her family, Europeans, had lived in Kenya for some time, and she worked in an office in Church house. She came to the Cathedral and for some time was in our house group. As we lived at the top of church house, she used to love to come up sometimes in her lunch hour and spend time with us. As I got to know her I learnt an important principle from her. She was in my kitchen sharing one day and said, "I know what you're thinking, you think I'm awful because..." "No," I said, "as a matter of fact I was counting the number of potatoes I was going to put in the pot. I wasn't thinking you were awful at all." How very important that we don't imagine what people are thinking, when most likely they are not. We can be spared some unintentional rejection.

Smartie Parties

In Kenya we also learnt about Mrs Smartie. "Mrs Smartie had a party, no one came. Mrs Smartie had another, just the same." We had many Smartie parties in Kenya. We would be expecting a group of Africans to come to Nairobi to stay with us for the weekend and we would buy all the food, and no one came. Nairobi might be bathed in sunshine but up-country there had been a rainstorm and the earth roads had turned into a quagmire and the buses couldn't move, nor could the people perhaps for two days. Alternatively, we wouldn't be expecting anyone, but there they would be.

A unique lady

After arriving in Kenya, one of the first people we met in Nairobi Cathedral was Mary Eyre. She was a tiny lady in her 60's whom David had met once in England. She said she had come out to Kenya to be the Lord's kitchen maid. She was Irish and had suffered rickets as a child and was somewhat bandy-legged. But her character and spirit meant she was a lady to be reckoned with. Straight away she advised us that we should take extra vitamins in Kenya.

It was Mary who told us of her meeting with an African Christian who had survived a 'Mau Mau' ordeal. Jomo Kenyatta and his thugs tried to force all Kikuyu people to drink a blood oath of loyalty to the tribe, or be killed. It was a strategy of fear. Mary asked this man what it had been like to be attacked in this way. He said, "I didn't feel anything at all. No pain. Only the most tremendous love for the people who were trying to kill me." Left for dead, somehow he survived and was able to witness to God's miraculous intervention.

Many Christians who faced such ordeals would say to their attackers, "We have symbolically drunk the blood of Jesus our Saviour. We have nothing against you and, if you kill us, we will go to be with Jesus. We would like you to know Jesus too, so that when you die you will go to be with him." Sometimes their attackers ran away in amazement at their lack of fear. Sometimes they killed them with their 'pangas', huge knives used for agriculture. Some Europeans were also caught up in this conflict and killed, but it was not primarily against Europeans.

Our ministry among the white farmers began with Neville Langford-Smith, Bishop of Nakuru inviting us to take part in a mission in Molo in which Mary played a vital role. This led on to him inviting us to give training in Bible discussion leading to settlers in other parts of his diocese, in Naivasha, Rongai and Nakuru where we met enthusiastic Christians, some of whom we are still in touch with.

It was a great joy to have time with George and Maureen Swannell. He was now the chaplain in Nakuru and years before, when he had been a curate in Crowborough, he had been such a help and encouragement to David when he was first a Christian.

I saw in Maureen a wonderful example of a godly wife and she has been such a special friend ever since.

An ordination and an accident

Towards the end of our time in Kenya we were invited to an African ordination service at Kitui, just over 100 miles each way on earth roads. Mary offered to drive us there and back. There was a spare seat in the car so I invited a friend whom I thought might particularly enjoy it. When I rang her, she said she had her flat to clean and wouldn't come after all. I thought she was mad to miss such a lovely opportunity. I thought I shouldn't press her into coming, as I easily could have done. We packed up picnics and several cars set off together. Archbishop Beecher was there with hundreds of Kamba under the shady Acacia trees. A makeshift communion table was set up with Seven-Up bottles as flower vases. It was such a privilege to share with African brothers and sisters in this meaningful ceremony.

After the ordination, four Europeans cars returned to Nairobi, stopping to picnic on the way. Mary was driving her Volkswagen Beetle towards the sun which was getting lower and being reflected in the recent rain puddles. Then a lorry came towards us on the single track of tarmac, so to share it we had to come halfway off onto the earth shoulder. In turning back onto the tarmac, the ridge tore off one of the front tubeless tyres. The car was out of control but I remember experiencing no fear or alarm. As the car rolled over onto its roof, a blanket of peace descended on me. I was the only one able to move and managed to get out.

David who had been in the back seat was now head first halfway out of the small side window which doesn't open. I remember calmly wondering if he was dying. His head was badly cut. Fortunately the car with two small children in it was ahead of us, so they never saw the accident. We were next, so the others behind were soon at the scene to help us, and then other cars came with two doctors on board. We were miles from anywhere.

Eventually an ambulance came and took David and Mary to Nairobi hospital, and I, with only a badly bruised leg and shock, was taken home by friends who put me to bed with much tender loving care. David joined me next day with only cuts on his head and slight concussion and shock. In the midst of it all we seemed to see only the miracles of God's providence, but the biggest was that my friend who wanted to clean her flat wasn't with us.

Sadly, Mary was paralysed from the neck down and was told she might have only 10 days to live, to which she replied, "Good, I will see the Lord all the sooner." In fact, she lived many more years. She didn't regain full mobility, but was wonderfully looked after in her house in Nairobi by loving Africans. Many would come to her bedside for counselling. And from her bed she would teach small boys how to climb the trees which she could see through her bedroom window.

We were very concerned that Mary's injuries were so much more serious than ours. But she said later that it would have broken her heart if we had been the ones more seriously hurt. Having been brought through death as it were, we felt even more committed to play our full part in whatever the Lord had planned for us in the future.

Kenya students studying abroad

Bartholomew's second son Sammy had the opportunity to study overseas. It was customary before departure to have a 'Harambee' or 'a pull-together party', when friends would bring gifts to help the student on his way. Bartholomew decided not to do this in case something went wrong and he, as a Christian, would be thought to have been getting money for his son under false pretences.

Sammy, with others from Kenya, went to East Germany but the students there wouldn't sit in the same classroom with black students. He was sent on to Moscow and had to learn Russian at the same time as beginning his engineering studies there. Soon the same thing happened; the Russian students wouldn't have Sammy or other Africans in their classes. So he sought help in the Kenyan Embassy. Fortuitously there was a group of American businessmen passing through, visiting various countries and travelling in a private jet, and they took Sammy with them as a kind of mascot.

Having visited many countries with him in Asia, they stopped in Rwanda on their way home and left Sammy with the Kenyan ambassador there. He then made his way back to Kenya on a series of buses. Sammy arrived home after only a few months abroad and with no degree. How wise Bartholomew had been not to accept 'Harambee' gifts.

We noticed that students coming back from America thought it must be much better to study in Russia, so they became anti-American. And those who got accepted by a Communist country thought it would have been much better in America, so they became anti-Communist. They were treated badly in both camps.

With Cyrus, Anna and the Howarths in Kiambu near Nairobi

With Evans, Esther and their children in Mwea near Mt Kenya

Attacking the 1st major rapid on the Ardèche in France

We took many Stewards' Trust ski parties to Zermatt

With Katya Trophimova and Sasha Popov in Ekaterinburg

From Murmansk 36 hours with Victor and Volodia

With brother Chris, niece Jo, and great-niece Jessie

With friends at another of Shirley's 80th parties

Saying goodbye to Kenya

The Navigators had initially asked us to go to Kenya for two years. Now they were asking us to stay on. It was a year after Kenya's Independence. David, praying on our flat roof as he often did, felt we shouldn't pray any more about it, because God had already attached his peace to us fulfilling our two years in Kenya and then returning to England.

The time came to tell people. Some thought we were running away after Kenyan independence, others asked us to join their organisations. But with peace in our hearts pointing us in only one direction, and my mother's age and illness in mind, we made our plans to depart. In the two years we were in Kenya, we met many people, both European and African, and a few Asians, and made some wonderful friends.

Church Army tea party

David had been the trainer of lay readers for the diocese of Nairobi and we had led training for Europeans in 5 centres in the diocese of Nakuru. Also we had led training in evangelism for the many different tribes represented at The Church Army college in Nairobi. The farewell tea party they gave us was very special. The students were sitting on both sides of two long tables. David was directed to one and I was directed to the other. At the end of tea, one of the students got up and made a speech to thank us. "Dear brother and Lady Steele," he began. That is the nearest I have been to acquiring a title, but I savour most the memory of that touching and sweet tea party.

David's class who gave the tea party

An extended homeward journey

This time, we would not be travelling by ship, but would be flying. Our plane ticket allowed us to add 5% more mileage to the most direct route and have stopovers. So we planned to visit Ethiopia, Lebanon, Jordan, Israel, Istanbul and Amsterdam.

Our early flight was to take off at 6am and kind friends drove us to Nairobi airport. To our amazement we found ninety people had come to see us off. One young man who was a teacher had travelled over 100 miles to do so. We found it so hard to tear ourselves away, especially from our African team and their families, whom we had come to know and love so much, even in such a comparatively short time. Such are the bonds of the Christian family worldwide that we belong to. I remember crying all day, I felt it so much.

Ethiopia and Sudan

We stayed one night in Addis Ababa in a missionary guesthouse, and the next day took a 20-seater plane one hour south to Soddu. As soon as I heard that there was a stop on the way, I thought, 'How nice, a chance of a cup of coffee.' In the event we landed in a field and there was nothing to be seen except a donkey and a lorry, so no coffee! We were back in rural Africa.

Dr Sheilds, whom we'd met with his family during a brief holiday south of Mombasa, had insisted that we visit them when we left Kenya. He was the doctor for a million people and his wife was the only qualified nurse. She had given birth to their fourth child only 4 days before we arrived. We had a fascinating two days and nights with them. They wanted to take us to a church. There were scarcely any roads, so mostly it was bumping along tracks in the bush. Suddenly with nothing in sight for miles, we came across an enormous mud and thatched hut in the shape of a huge beehive and inside hundreds of black and smiling faces already there. Our time with them was an eye-opener. Then our doctor host drove us 8 hours back to Addis, combining it with his monthly visit to replenish stores and medicines.

Our next stop-over was Khartoum where, while staying with Brian and Gill Lea, we met up with a student worker, Christine White, who'd been in our youth group in Sevenoaks. She whisked us off to a picnic, a talk and a game of football on the battle site of Omdurman. David's shoes only just survived.

The Middle East, Turkey & Holland

In Lebanon we stayed with a Navigator staff member, and met some of his university contacts whom he'd first got to know as boys by playing monopoly with them.

Jordan

The Navigators in Lebanon had recently had a mission in Jerusalem and suggested we visit the photography shop near the Jaffa gate as the young assistant photographer there had become a Christian. David went and met him, and was invited to a Bible study in the Armenian quarter that evening. There he met an Air Liban pilot, the young photographer and others, and a carpenter next to him, who said, "We're starting again at Jerusalem." It was very inspiring.

It was 1965, before The Six Day War, so The Old City was still all in Jordan. There was no contact at all between Jordan and Israel so we couldn't contact our Finnish friend in Israel until after we had walked, carrying our suitcases, through 'no man's land'. And we had to have separate passports to visit Israel. In Jordon, we stayed in the compound of St George's English church and visited many biblical sites in the city such as the Wailing Wall, the Upper Room, the Way of Sorrows, the Holy Sepulchre Church, and outside the city, Gordon's Calvary, the Garden Tomb and the Mount of Olives. We also visited Bethlehem, Jacob's Well and the sights around Galilee. At night we could see Syrian gunfire from the Golan Heights.

It was so good to see the biblical sites in their real surroundings and the stony ground that Jesus spoke of in the parable of the sower, and the lilies of the field and find they were anemones, also to see the Golden Gate blocked up against Jesus Christ's return and know that would be in vain, because one day he would return and walk through it and no one could stop him.

Israel

On the other side of no man's land, we found our Finnish friend Kija Mya working with Jewish people. She later married and lived in the States and continued to work with Israelis.

Turkey

In Istanbul we visited Haghia Sophia, the Blue Mosque and the Grand Bazaar. We had a first class guide around a fascinating museum which had been the Shah's Palace. The exhibition of jewels seemed even more magnificent than our own crown jewels.

Holland

In Amsterdam, we had a refreshing time with Gien Karssen, Manny and Eric and other Navigator staff, whom we had met earlier on Navigator conferences and missions. From their loving care we made our last lap to London to a heartwarming reception by English Navigator staff, and then home to families, and to whatever lay ahead.

Back in England - a special car

My mother came through the illness she had in our absence, but now she needed more care and was in a nursing home nearby. We were able to base ourselves with my father in my parents' home. Our first need was a car. A second-hand Vauxhall Viva seemed the most suitable. We especially wanted windows in the back that opened, which didn't seem possible with this model. When we were asked what colour we would like we said, "Blue." "Lord," we asked, "we would like a Viva with back windows that open." Eventually the garage tracked down a second-hand one for us and came back to us apologetically. "We are so sorry, they said, "it's blue, but it has windows in the back that open." That particular model usually didn't. This was another lesson on praying specifically. Specific answers are so very encouraging. Our heavenly father loves to answer his children's prayers.

The car's number plate was HPB so we called it 'Happy People Back'. Years later when we needed a more powerful car to pull our caravan for Purpose Holidays, Maurice Wood, principal of Oak Hill College, wrote to David to ask if any of the members of the Stewards' Trust would like to contribute towards a car for George Carey, one of their lecturers. Instead of trading in our Viva, we asked if George would like it. When we delivered it to him at Oak Hill, we said that there was just one condition - they had to have the name that went with it.

Many years later when George Carey was Archbishop of Canterbury, Lambeth Palace became open to the public on certain days, so we took the opportunity to see it. While we were enjoying tea in a marquee in the garden afterwards, George came in with a group and I happened to catch his eye. As he turned towards us he said, "I hope you are enjoying your visit?" I replied, "Happy People Back." His eyes lit up as he recognized us, and he later introduced his wife Eileen to us again. "We saw that model of the Viva only the other day and were thinking of you," she said. You never know whom you might be helping next.

Hospitality in the kitchen

One of the first things we did on returning from Kenya was to stand in for the rector of St Nicholas Sevenoaks, our old parish, while he was on a well-earned 6 week holiday. It was a new experience to live in someone else's home and observe life in a vicarage from the inside. It was a good base for us and we were able to welcome the Sheild family and their four children coming on furlough via England en route to the States. It was the May bank holiday weekend I remember, and I was feeling some trepidation at the thought of feeding nine over the weekend instead of just the two of us.

It was such a pleasure to see them again after our stay with them in Ethiopia two months earlier. It was on their first day with us that I was struggling to get lunch in the McLellan's unfamiliar rather long and thin kitchen. My attitude in a kitchen was always that I really had to have it to myself to make a meal or I couldn't cope. First, the elder girl of 12 came in. She wanted to clean out the birdcage and began to do it. Then the youngest boy of four came in, his question was, "How does the kettle boil without any fire under it?" Mother then arrived and settled herself in a chair to feed the baby and wanted to talk. Next their 8-year-old son appeared from somewhere and settled himself at the table, and last but not least father (doctor to a million southern Soddu Ethiopians), not wanting to be left out in the cold, arrived with his book.

My stress level had been rising as each one had arrived to join in the fun. They just wanted to be with me in the kitchen, so who was I to say they shouldn't be there because I thought I couldn't cope? I offered up a silent prayer of capitulation, "Sorry Lord, I'm never again going to say I have to have the kitchen to myself to provide a meal." I just got on with it and worked over their heads and somehow meals for 8 to 9 were successfully achieved, and I enjoyed this lovely family and the privilege of having them.

During that summer opportunities for helping other churches with training courses came too, and with our new-to-us Viva we were free to respond.

Helpful Hints

Washing up liquid

We use a lot of washing-up liquid in our homes. For economy, save your last empty washing-up liquid bottle. When you buy a new one transfer one third of it into the old bottle and fill up with water. The solution is weaker, but probably quite adequate with an extra squirt from time to time. It will also save that surfeit of bubbles in the bowl and your washing-up liquid will go three times as far, saving many pennies over a period of a year. Keep the new bottle to dilute by half next time a fill-up is needed.

Window cleaning

There are many special window cleaners on the market. But they are expensive, especially if your windows are rather large. Half a bucket of hot water with the small squeeze of washing-up liquid and a tablespoon of vinegar will do the job just as well. Finish off with scrunched up newspaper, and you'll have more pennies in your pocket and sparkling windows.

Helpful Hints

A burnt saucepan

That smell of burning, that anticipation of getting it clean, that sinking feeling, can now be a thing of the past.

A tablespoon of vinegar in hot water, soak overnight and the rest is easy.

Washing paintwork

A painter once told me the secret of washing paint. Never work from the top down, as you'll never get rid of those 'runs' down the paint. Always wash from the bottom upwards and you will never have that problem.

Polishing furniture

Prepare your surface by first wiping over the table with a damp cloth wrung out in water with a dash of vinegar added. This will remove grease and marks off the surface. Put the polish on against the grain for greater penetration. Leave for a short while. When polishing off, polish gently with the grain for the best results.

A mother's wisdom

In Scotland in the early 1920s children living in the country would walk to school and back, sometimes several miles. There was one small boy, who decided he didn't want to go to school, and that nobody would know. There were no telephones there in those days, so the school wouldn't be ringing up his home to find out where he was. They would most likely presume that he was unwell or something like that.

Eventually another parent told his mother that he wasn't going to school, but was off doing his own thing. His mother told her son what the other mother had reported about him not attending school and then added, "But I didn't believe her because you wouldn't do such a thing like that." That small boy never absconded from school again. It was he who told us this when in his 70s.

Chaplain to the Stewards' Trust

During that summer David was invited to become chaplain to The Stewards' Trust. It had started when two Oxford undergraduates, John Bickersteth, later David's best man, and Michael Alison, who had been studying the Bible together with John Reynolds, a college don, left to start work in London. He encouraged them to continue studying the Bible and invite their friends and relations to join them. As they grew they divided into more groups, meeting in different members' flats. As part of their living as Christians, and in order to encourage each other to take a responsible attitude to their finances and to Christian giving, they called themselves The Stewards' Trust.

At the committee that interviewed us we found that we already knew 11 of the 13 present. David was appointed chaplain and Tom Watts was asked to help us find a flat in the middle of London, where most of them were living. By that time they had multiplied to become 30 groups, so there were about 300 members. At the request of Michael Alison, who was by then an M.P., the Bishop of London agreed to license David to do this work, without having the added responsibility of being attached to a particular local church. A second-floor flat in 16 Bolton gardens became our home and base from which to work among them for the next eight years. What a welcome they gave us and what friends we became. By 1972 they had multiplied to 600.

Dealing with disappointment

We had recently returned from working in Kenya to a new home in London, in the middle of all the young people's flats with whom we were going to be working. While we were abroad, we had lent our furniture, in two lots, to others and were now receiving it back, to make our own home in England again. One lot came back undamaged, but the other lot came back with considerable damage done, even a particularly favourite laundry basket had been painted a different colour, which couldn't be rectified.

When our friends and mentors Doug and Leila Sparks came to supper and she asked me how I was, I remember saying, "discouraged." "Let me tell you where discouragement leads to" she said, "discouragement leads to depression and depression leads to despair".

This rang a bell in my mind as I listened. "Discouragement comes from doubt and doubt comes from disappointment" she said, and drew this diagram:

disappointment
    doubt
        discouragement
            depression
                despair

As I thought about it, I realised this was very true for me and could be like a spiral which I could go down very quickly.

The least little thing that disappointed me could send me down to despair. The question was, what was I going to do about it? I decided I couldn't just do nothing, so instead of going to church the next Sunday, I spent time on my own thinking about this diagram and how it applied to me.

From the present time I began to name the disappointments I felt. "Lord I'm calling them disappointments, but I'm really doubting you in the situation. I am sorry." Back and back I went, until I found myself telling God of an instance five years earlier. I had at last realised that I was jealous of someone. I had acknowledged the jealousy as wrong, but I was dogged by the disappointment that someone had made me jealous, and it seemed the devil could make havoc of my emotions with this disappointment. I could be ironing in Africa and I would suddenly think of this situation and become discouraged and depressed. When I named all these things before the Lord and apologised for them, it was like having a spiritual bath and I was clean from them all. The devil no longer had a hold on me through them, and couldn't send me down the spiral, especially with the problem of the jealousy.

Now when I recognize disappointment I confess it quickly and don't let it lead to doubt and discouragement, so I don't go down the spiral. We are told in Romans 8:28 that "All things work together for good to those who love the Lord" and this certainly includes disappointments large or small. Years later I discovered that particular little laundry basket that had been painted blue, fitted exactly with the material I had for making curtains for our present bathroom. There is nothing unredeemable. All things work together for good to those who love the Lord.

The same applied in our ministry among the members of the Stewards' Trust.

Without children to give away our ages which, as time passed became nearer to their parents ages than to theirs, we were free to be with them at any time or place: to have them into our home, to go to theirs, to be with them wherever they went, to help them to mature in their new walk with their new-found saviour Jesus Christ and find out his purposes for them. Even childlessness worked together for good.

Ashburnham and weddings

During the year we would have six teaching weekends at Ashburnham Place, a large mansion with beautiful formal gardens inherited by John Bickersteth, one of the founders of the Stewards' Trust and chairman of the committee. He had prayed for 5 years to know what to do with it, and had concluded that God wanted him to make it into a Christian Conference Centre. He became the first director. These weekends played a huge part in the lives of the members later in life. When married and moved out of London they expressed their gratitude for the foundation and help they had received as they now tried to play their part in local parish life.

Their ages were 17 to 35 and soon they were going to meet their partners for life. And many of them did marry those they met in the Stewards' Trust groups. In the eight years we were with them David took 150 weddings up and down the country. He was the clergyman that most of them knew best.

They were our family, and we are grateful to still be in touch with many of them as, in their turn, their children are getting married and having their children. And they are passing on their values and their knowledge of Jesus Christ to new generations.

Shirley's ducks

We also took advantage of conferences organised by other groups. One such was a Navigator weekend for girls in the midlands. I was able to take a group to it, but I soon discovered that there were two different cultures clashing. My group, so confident in West London, were suddenly thrown off balance, not quite knowing what to do, and followed me around like ducklings. From that time on this group became known as 'Shirley's ducks'. They used to meet regularly in our flat for Bible discussions.

I had an uncle who had retired to Portugal, and he would visit us in London each summer. He became fascinated by the ducklings and would always want to visit our flat when they were there. He eventually became known as 'The Honourable Donald' and was allowed to have supper with us, but not join our meeting.

We became quite strict with ourselves and agreed to make our Tuesday evenings an absolute priority, to put in and get the most out of them, and to provide continuity. This sometimes got tested to the limit, when for example Aunt Mary turned up in London with two theatre tickets, and someone had to say "No" to Aunt Mary, who couldn't understand at all why they couldn't come. But much was learnt about commitment and priority.

Blessing through skiing

We joined the Stewards' Trust in October 1965 and discovered that one of their favourite holidays was to go skiing. Shortly before Easter, we realised that if we didn't take a holiday then we wouldn't get one until October, so we began to think, holiday - fresh air - exercise, what about skiing? David had never skied, although I had with my family years ago. I thought my skiing days were over. I had learnt to ski in Zermatt which was one of the few resorts high enough to still have enough snow at Easter. It seemed the place to aim for. And if we could learn to ski, we would be able to ski with our 'new family' and maybe use it in some way in the future.

I had heard that the Commonwealth and Continental Church Society sent ministers to holiday resorts. David phoned them and came back to the kitchen laughing his head off. The conversation went something like this, "I am an Anglican Minister, could you use me at Easter?" "What country are you interested in?" "Switzerland." "Just a minute.... we haven't sent a chaplain to Zermatt since the typhoid epidemic, would you like to go there?" David was laughing. Because, as he said, "Who but the Lord would send you to the only place you wanted to go to?"

There was a knock on our door one day, and there stood Pom with a pair of skis, her ski jacket and an envelope full of francs to buy a ski pass. We were well launched and set off. We felt we must take this as a real holiday, but also prayed that we would each meet someone would want to know Jesus that year.

It was 10 years since I had last been in Zermatt. The sun was shining, and the village and lack of cars and the view of the Matterhorn looked as lovely as ever. As we walked up the village street to find our hotel, we had hardly got halfway there when there was Arthur coming down towards us. "Hello Shirley," he said. He had been my ski teacher all those years before and I hadn't seen him since!

Togged up and ready to go, off we went to the ski school. "I haven't skied for 10 years," I said. "Go back to class one," they said. We joined Emille on the nursery slopes. By lunchtime he said, "You have skied before." So I got promoted to class 2. In class 2 they said, "You have skied before." So I got promoted again, this time to a completely different mountain from David.

When not in class, David and I had fun trying to stay on the drag lifts and practice what we were been taught, which was a whole new way of skiing from my earlier days, lifting up into the turn instead of the long low sweep as we bent down into the turn. Having lunch one day on the same mountain for once, David looked at a girl and said to me, "She was in church this morning and seemed very moved." On the crowded train up to Rotenboden I managed to get alongside her. "I believe you were in church this morning," I said. "Yes," she said, "I'm a Buddhist." Not expecting much response, I said, "We could talk some more if you would like to." "When?" she said emphatically. So we planned a time, and shared an ice cream and the gospel together.

She didn't make the next planned meeting, so I thought I had lost her, and she was leaving Zermatt in a few days. A couple of days later we were skiing when the light turned bad, so we had to come down to the village as we couldn't see on the mountain. We were sitting in a cafe window having hot chocolates when my new friend walked past on her way to the station. I ran out and we exchanged addresses. She found Jesus that year and we have remained friends to this day.

David found himself having lunch with an Englishman one day, who came from London. David asked him if he went to church. When he replied that he did, David asked him if there were many Christians in his church. "They're all Christians," he replied. "How amazing," David said, "I've never known a church where they were all Christians." "Well, what you mean by a Christian then?" What a splendid question to be asked. The two of them met often after that, and he too found Jesus that summer.

We were greatly encouraged by these two answers to our prayers and saw how skiing could lead to many meetings with people who might be searching for the meaning of life. Since then we have led many groups of Stewards' Trust members to meet and help others on the ski slopes. Behind a smiling face there may be a stressed marriage, a failing business and one of many other problems that can cause someone to welcome a helpful Christian coming alongside.

Mogul Mice

One Christmas we had a chalet full of people having coffee after the morning service. There were some younger children there about 5 or 6-years-old, and I found myself delegated to tell them a story. Not having children of my own I really didn't know any, so I began to make one up.

I was standing by the trees on a run one day when I suddenly heard a small voice say, "Excuse me?" I looked down to find myself looking at Mr Mogul Mouse. "Excuse me?" he said, "I'm awfully hungry. Do you have a nut?" "Yes," I said, "I always carry nuts in my waist bag." He was so grateful and asked if I would like to come to their cheese feast. They live under the moguls which are snow mounds made by many skiers turning in the same place. The lady Mogul Mice wear pink aprons with white spots on. They manufacture diamonds and, if you're very lucky and catch the early train up the Gornergrat railway, you may see where they have laid out diamonds to dry on the snow.

A lady who heard me telling this story went home and tried to look them up in her bird book.

One day I went up the Gornergrat railway in the late morning. There were two mothers distraught with children rushing about all over the place. I thought it was time to tell a Mogul Mouse story to the seven-year-old boy and his five-year-old sister. As I did so, he looked out of the window. "There, I saw one," he said. His little sister looked out also, "I saw one too." "Really," I said, what were they doing?" "Getting married," she said, "with diamonds in their hair."

Peter was the grandson of Mr and Mrs Nixon. He came to me one day with two sugar lumps. "Will you give these to Mr Mogul Mouse please," he said. "How many meals will they last Mr Mogul Mouse do you think?" We had a long conversation about how many grains of sugar he might eat at each meal, to try to determine how long these two sugar lumps would last him. I didn't see Peter again for many years, until we happened to meet at Heathrow, flying to Geneva on the same plane. "Do you remember the Steeles?" his father said. "No," he replied, "but I remember the Mogul Mice."

In the summer the Mogul Mice hitch lifts to Italy on the log lorries, where they help with the harvest in Rudipuglia and Poggibonzo, and make blueberry jam and bring it back to the mountains for the winter.

Seconded to other organisations

During our time with the Stewards' Trust, they kindly lent us to other organisations from time to time, like theological colleges such as Oak Hill and St John's, Nottingham.

The longest was for 3 months in 1966 to the Billy Graham organisation before and during his 'Greater London Crusade'. Billy Graham wanted to help the churches with a new way of following up the new Christians. David was asked to prepare a suitable training course.

So he wrote the course notes and then trained 5, who in turn trained 50, who in turn each trained 2 groups of 10. These 1,000 then went back to their churches to train others. By this simple multiplication, such as the Holy Spirit urged and blessed in the early church, just three months later about 30,000 people were meeting to study, discuss and apply the Bible in their daily lives, and unbelievers were coming to know Christ through these groups too. The next year 45,000 more started meeting in such groups in the 22 other cities where Billy Graham's 'All England Crusade' was relayed.

John Pollock, author of 'Crusade 66' wrote, "And thus was born what may prove one of the most significant developments of the entire London crusade — the Bible discussion groups training programme."

Until that time very few churches had small groups where discussion took place or applications were shared.

Quite early on in our time with the Stewards' Trust, CWR were running a week long conference at Butlin's holiday camp in Minehead. The chalets would have been more inviting in hot midsummer rather than in chilly early spring. David was asked to lead a training course in how to share your faith, as one of the optional seminars. We were allocated a large hall as 200 people had chosen to attend.

There were no overhead projectors in those days, so as David went through the 'Bridge to Life' diagram with a volunteer on the front of the platform, I had to be also on the platform walking about behind them, and simultaneously copying onto a large board beside them whatever David drew or wrote. I was glad to be agile in those days.

The sessions included how to talk with people and listen for their needs, how to share one's own story, how to show them in the Bible the good news of what Jesus has done for us, and how to help people understand the response God is looking for, so that they can begin a relationship with him. David never leads such training without taking those on the course out to meet real people, either in the street or in their homes. So with the permission of local ministers, all 200 were invited to come out in pairs soon after lunch that day to go house to house or talk with people in the streets of Minehead and the nearby villages.

At the end of the morning session an extra large lady came to him to say that she was far too nervous to come out that afternoon. David said that the best thing to do, if you have butterflies in your stomach is to feed them well, so have a good lunch. And then remember that you're not going out alone, you're going with a fellow Christian, and with God the Holy Spirit. He impressed on her that she would benefit so much from the experience if she came out with us. Bravely she did. And what happened?

She and her partner knocked on the door of the first house in the row that they had been allocated. A lady opened it and said, "I have a retarded child," as if to say, "God isn't interested in me". To which the extra large lady replied, "I have a retarded child too."

We were told later that day that both visitors were immediately invited in and had a very worthwhile conversation over a cup of tea. And the large lady said to David, "This has been the best afternoon of my life." Her bravery was rewarded and the one they visited was blessed too. What a joy it is to see again and again that God is no man's debtor.

Another organisation who asked for training in Bible discussion group leading was Campus Crusade, for their 1971 European staff conference. The two of us would train 10 each during the first week and then each of them would train 10 others during the second week, and then David would train the country leaders. In this way all 220 and the leaders would receive the training. I remember feeling incredibly scared of doing this and would willingly have run away, but couldn't. In the event, one couldn't have had a more attentive group, because they were going to have to train others during the second week.

Somehow over the previous months I had heard negative things about this group which had built up in my mind. I remember being so ashamed of these negative thoughts when I discovered that they never said a negative word about any other organisation. It left an indelible mark in my mind. They were some of the sweetest women I have ever met.

Leaving the Stewards' Trust

We had eight wonderful years with the Stewards' Trust and came to know many so well. We had training courses, holiday weekends, and countless times with individuals and the group leaders, as they in turn sought to help the group members. In some ways we were their London parents and in others their mentors. Sometimes we were shoulders to cry on, sometimes there to share good news. Many came to breakfast, some came when we had our dressing gowns on ready for bed.

Eventually, the committee felt it was time for a change and we had to dig ourselves out of this family that had become so much a part of us and move on. It was a sort of bereavement because of the close involvement with so many.

The next step was an invitation to join the Commonwealth and Continental Church Society to do something in the package holiday resorts on the Mediterranean coast. They were able to buy the flat in 16 Bolton gardens from the Stewards' Trust, so we felt frightfully special having a flat bought twice for us, and very grateful to remain there and not to have to move.

More training in Finland

That December David had been asked by Kalevi Lehtinen to lead a training weekend in 'Sharing Your Faith' for 70 young Finish Lutheran ministers - staff evangelists and others. It was held at the headquarters of the Peoples Bible Society at Vivamo, near Helsinki, where they also have a beautiful conference centre beside a lake. This allows Finns, between visits to the hot room of the sauna, to swim in freezing water with a beautiful view.

David feels that one of the most important parts of his training is giving people practical experience of going out in pairs to talk with real strangers. On this occasion, after the initial training, they went out into the streets and homes of the nearby town, something they had never done before, a completely new experience for them. They were not allowed to wear their clerical collars and had to be incognito to talk to people. As we didn't speak Finnish we couldn't go out with them so stayed to welcome them back at the end of the afternoon to hear their stories.

As we welcomed back the pairs from their afternoon adventure before gathering to share how they had all got on, I passed the director of Vivamo outside her house crying. When I asked her what was the matter she said, "It's their faces, their faces, seeing the shining faces of those returning. I've never seen anything like it."

Two of them met a girl who was astonished to find people talking about Christianity in the street. She said to the two of them, "I thought Christians stayed at home knitting socks for missionaries."

One agreed conclusion at the end of the weekend was, that as evangelists they would never lead missions again without training others in how to talk to people personally about Jesus. This particular training added a new dimension to their lives and to their vision. So we were very thankful to the Lord for using this training and experience to help them.

Kenya and South Africa

It was suggested we should take a sabbatical between jobs, so we were able to revisit Kenya, and go on to South Africa to a congress and my father's 80th birthday, and then return to England briefly before spending some weeks in Canada and the USA.

It was a joy to be back in Kenya again, visiting our team, meeting their children eight years on, and sharing their lives and joys and sorrows and stories. We were able to lead courses in Bible discussion group leading there, some of whose members are still passing on, 35 years later, what they learnt then.

We were invited by African Enterprise to take part in the Durban Congress on Evangelism culminating in Billy Graham speaking at a huge rally. It was the first time that the Apartheid Government had allowed all races to stay in the same hotel and sit anywhere they liked in the stadium. These were conditions that Billy Graham specified before he would come to speak.

The Congress gave an opportunity for several smaller seminars, and because David had brought his course notes with him, he was asked to train those who chose the personal evangelism seminar. After training, he took them out in pairs into the streets in Durban to talk to people about Jesus.

One of the delegates from Zimbabwe was Chris, a detective inspector and a two-year-old Christian. The first person he and his partner met in the street was a South African detective inspector. Chris was able to help him to know more about Jesus. When he returned to Harare, he wrote to David and said he had started the TIC-TOC club, standing for 'Take In Criminals - Turn Out Christians'. He later joined African Enterprise and led their Fox Fire teams, and after that he became the Alpha coordinator for Zimbabwe.

We met many other Christian leaders and had an hour alone with Billy Graham, who was very interested to hear about the Stewards' Trust ministry in London.

Another whom we met was Gordon Scutt's aunt. She had been a missionary in Swaziland for many years already. Directly after the Congress she drove us to her home there with Mrs 'Crocodile', who was a very large lady with whom I shared the back seat of the car. She was determined that I should master the Swazi word for 'good day'. Every so often she would say the word very slowly and get me to repeat it. Without perhaps realising it, she was fulfilling one of the laws of memorising - repetition. After eight hours in the car I had learnt 'Sagabona', and I remember it to this day.

Next, at Bishop Zulu's request, David led his training course in evangelism for 45 Zulu and white clergy in Melmoth. Being David's helper with visual aids and other things seemed to make a huge impression on the Zulu clergy.

Finally, we stayed with Michael and Carol Cassidy in Pietermaritzburg, where David trained 10 African Enterprise staff in Bible Discussion Group leading.

After this we hoped to get 1,000 miles west to Cape Town by Easter for my father's 80th birthday, but we had no idea how. Soon we were the recipients of a God-given arrangement. After the course at Michael Cassidy's house we met a businessman, Vic Pierce, who when he heard of our need, said that he planned to drive there by Easter but didn't want to go alone, so please would we come with him!

At the Congress many people had pressed pieces of paper into our hands with their names and addresses on, saying, "Please come and visit us." As we pooled all these pieces of paper and laid them on the table, many of them were right on our route and Vic knew all but one. When we rang that person, the mother of someone in one of the Stewards' Trust groups in London, and told her who was driving us, she said, "That's the one person my 19-year-old house guest wants to discuss his future career with, how wonderful."

One coloured curate, said he was hesitant to invite us to visit him. Because he said, "My wife will spit at you." They had been one of many coloured communities whose whole neighbourhood had been moved by the apartheid government out of their homes to nothing but a field and some empty tents. We said, "We will come anyway." She didn't spit at us, and because I was also a curate's wife we had much in common. Respecting and loving her, broke down some of the barriers and she ended up making us sandwiches for our onward journey. We prayed together and hugged each other. We were so glad we had risked possible rejection and could bring some Christian love to her. And Vic made a great impression among the kids in the local school as he talked with them about the difference that Jesus could make to their lives.

Before flying from Jo'burg on our way back to Kenya, we were driven up past Pretoria to give training to Methodists of the Sotho tribe near Phalaborwa. They sang and danced most beautifully at every opportunity and taught us to join in with them between sessions, before and after meals, in and out of church, and at every other possible moment. It was a very special lilting tune, and they were surprised that we could pick up the dance rhythm and steps so quickly.

Back in Kenya, what a joy it was to revisit our former team members and see how they were doing, and lead some more training courses in Nairobi and Nakuru.

Canada and the USA

Pirrko, who had been teaching dance for a year in Chicago, met us at Toronto airport at midnight. We pitched our tent by the lights of her car. It being a wide American car, she slept along the front bench seat. After driving along the Gaspé Peninsular to Prince Edward Island, there we got the last 3 tickets for the last performance of 'Anne of Green Gables', her favourite childhood book. We returned along the coast of Maine to New York for her to ship her car to Finland, and then the three of us spent another valuable week at a 'Basic Youth Conflicts' conference in Philadelphia.

After this David and I visited friends in California and Colorado before heading north over the border to visit another friend in Calgary. Finally we trickled happily home, leading courses in Toronto, Kingston and Montreal for university students and nurses connected to Inter-Varsity.

Purpose Holidays by the Med

In 1973 David, who had been for several years chairing the Intercontinental Church Society committee concerned with ministry to holidaymakers, was invited to join the staff and do something for the British visitors in the new package holiday resorts in Spain. There were no English churches in these resorts nor would holidaymakers be looking for a church, so new thinking was needed to take the good news of Jesus to the thousands going there from Britain for their two-week summer holiday. 'Holidays with a Purpose', later changed to 'Purpose Holidays', was born. So David trained teams from universities and churches to meet people in the hotels and campsites, in the lounges and bars, and around the swimming pools and talk with them about Jesus.

In 1973 the British consul-general in Barcelona had told David it would be all right to talk with people in the streets, but when we arrived in Spain the next summer, with our first team following, David was told by Salvador, the officer for tourism in Lloret de Mar, that if more than 19 people gathered in the street all would be put in prison. So where could we meet Brits? Just as the unbelieving Persian king Cyrus helped Ezra and the Israelite exiles to return to Jerusalem, so Salvador helped us.

He suggested asking 4 hotel managers if we could talk with their British guests. All four agreed, as did 8 of the other 9 where Brits were staying in Lloret that summer. So each team had over 3,000 Brits they could visit within 10 minutes walk. This became quite the best way of meeting Brits in all the resorts that Purpose Holiday teams subsequently visited. After supper they were usually sitting at tables or in hotel lounges with plenty of time and in no hurry to do anything else.

Lloret de Mar was our first resort, Then, as the numbers of teams grew, we added Sitges, Pineda, Salou and Benidorm, then in Italy, Lido di Jesolo and Catholica, then Porec in Yugoslavia. then Corfu, then Magalluf in Majorca and San Antonio in Ibiza. Finally we added the largest campsite in France, Prairies de la Mer, near St Tropez. That summer we had 300 Christians in 30 teams taking part.

To orientate the teams to their resorts when they arrived, we would need to be out there ourselves. So we set off to the Caravan Show that year to find a suitable caravan in which to live. We imagined we could make our decision very quickly and be back home by mid-morning. In practice we found Earl's Court Arena swimming in caravans like sheep, all looking exactly the same to us. At the end of the day, having had one sandwich and a glass of milk, we were exhausted and no nearer knowing what we wanted or needed.

Weeks later the problem was resolved, and we became the proud owners of a second-hand 2-berth Welton Galliard quality caravan, which was to be our home in Europe for the next 20 summers as the work developed, and as we travelled around meeting the teams in Spain, France, Italy and Yugoslavia. A team leader gave us a picture to put up in the caravan above the book shelf. Its caption is, 'Blessed are those who wander with the Lord'.

Caravan maintenance for Purpose Holidays

Each spring David would comb through the British tour operators' summer brochures to see where Brits would be staying. He and each team leader would then decide which resort their team would go to.

Of course we didn't expect people to go abroad to share their faith without any training. Sometimes David led the training where the teams came from. For 12 years we also had training weekends in London in the church hall of Holy Trinity Brompton. HTB was our church at that time. One year 200 needed to be fed over a weekend, so I was very grateful to have many helpers.

After interactive sessions on sharing your experience, explaining the gospel and listening, each Saturday afternoon of the weekend we'd go out in pairs into The Brompton Road and the surrounding streets to meet people. I remember hearing how one pair met a Muslim girl who asked them, "Can Jesus help me to slim? She was rightly told, "Yes, but you'd have to know him first."

As well as many stories of worthwhile conversations, the consensus was, "We'd no idea people were so interested." So the team members were greatly encouraged that their Purpose Holiday would, in a few months' time, be enjoyed by them and also be appreciated by those they went to help.

Then David and I would set out with the caravan, ahead of the first team, for him to visit all the hotel managers in their resort where Brits would be staying, to ask their permission for one or two pairs to visit their English speaking guests in the evenings.

In Italy, where the resort hotels are much smaller than in Spain, 69 of the 70 hotel managers in Lido di Jesolo, where Brits were staying, said, "Yes." After a few years of knowing them, one manager said to David, "Seven in the morning until two o'clock the next morning do whatever you like. This is your home."

I loved the visiting, the simple outdoor lifestyle, meals outside, team Bible discussions under our awning, taking one's washing 'to the well' for a cold water hand wash, hanging it on lines between trees, getting to know the neighbours and the campsite staff, who acquired nicknames and became friends, despite our lack of mutual language.

Clothes pegs and picnics

Clothes pegs proved to be more valuable than diamonds in all the tasks they were put to, and we loved the simple life of camping and living in the outdoors. The picnic basket was worth its weight in gold and thermoses were always filled ready for stops on our travels. Purpose Holidays are on hold, but the picnic habit remains with us, and there is hardly a journey when it doesn't accompany us ready for a coffee stop or a lunch break. As we pray about each day and ask for God's guidance that we might be a blessing to others, two occasions stand out when our picnic basket was at the ready.

On one journey we pulled into the car park of a country park unknown to us before. We had hardly parked when out of the gate walked a friend, James Broad. We hadn't seen him for a very long time and were thrilled to see him. It turned out that he had been having a quiet day with God in this peaceful place, but expressed his dismay that the kiosk he was depending on for food and drink was closed, so he had not even had a cup of tea. "James" we said, "We have tea and food, picnic tables and chairs, do join us". As Archbishop William Temple used to say, "When I pray coincidences happen, when I don't they don't."

On another occasion we were travelling to Ashburnham and decided to stop for a picnic on the cliffs at Bexhill. I remember thinking that morning, "Fill both thermoses and that will give us 3 cups each, if we want them". So I piled in the cakes and buns, knowing it was far more than we needed. We parked and found a bench in a wonderful position with a great view of the sea where we could have our picnic. David went back to the car for the picnic basket and to my surprise returned with a good friend, Marigold, whom we'd not seen for several years. She was sitting in the car parked next to ours and had come down to the cliffs to get a taste of sea air. The tea was more than enough, and we spent an hour or so catching up and sharing news, much encouraged by the coincidental meeting, or was it?

Playing with dolphins

Pirkko, after leaving London, returned to her teaching career in Finland. Some years later she heard of a two-year missionary training scheme run by Agape in London. After three months with them, she was assigned to Portugal for 18 months. She learned the language and worked among families in the mountains outside Oporto.

On one of her many visits from Finland to Portugal after she became a missionary there, she stopped by with us in Lloret de Mar. Discovering that she had never seen a live dolphin, she and I paid a visit to the local dolphinarium. After the show we were intrigued to watch a class of small children controlled by their teacher. She placed each small hand on opposite sides of a rope, side by side, one pair behind another, and they were led away in line like a snake. They were chattering away and not looking where they were going, as children are wont to do, but perfectly safe as they were led along firmly attaching themselves to the rope.

By this time we were almost the last out of the arena. As we neared the gate, we passed a small pool with a mother and baby dolphin in it and one of the performing ones had been let in there too. There was a human family on the side of the pool throwing a ball to the performing dolphin, who was throwing it back to them. When the family left, I wondered what the dolphin would do. He started playing ball with us, one of life's very nicest experiences.

Flowers on the table and green soap

Whether it was high season or not I don't remember, but it was evening and we were tired and we came to Camping Eden, and there was a 'Full' notice on the gate. But we were desperate and thought we would go into the office and see if they could squeeze us in somewhere for one night. They took us in for one night. The next day we went back to the office and they thought they would be able to have us for another few days. It was an Englishman and his Belgian wife who were running the campsite, which turned out to be rather exclusive. They always kept the 'full' notice at the entrance because they only took in people they liked the look of, and we somehow got into that category and became good friends, and returned on our journeys home for several years after that.

The following day, as our neighbours went off for a day out, we noticed on the back of their car a big 'Suomi' Finland label, so we put a vase of flowers on their table. When they came back they were puzzled about the flowers, so we introduced ourselves and told of our links with Finland. We invited them over for lemonade, and Maija-Liisa and her two sons came and we had a good time with them.

A day or two later I had a shower, and on returning to the caravan realised I'd left my piece of green soap in the shower block. What may be of little value at home becomes of immense value on a campsite, and such was my piece of soap. When we finished our supper I returned to the shower block to look for it, and there I met Maija-Liisa and we got talking. It soon transpired that she was a Christian. When we had introduced ourselves originally she had wondered if perhaps we were also, because no Finn would dream of introducing themselves like that.

She was extremely unhappy, going through a very difficult time with her husband, who was totally against her Christian faith. She was desperate to talk to someone who understood. So here we were in the privacy of the women's shower block where she could cry her heart out and share her difficulties with a fellow Christian, who could love her and comfort her, and it was all because of a piece of green soap.

We met her several different years on Camping Eden, and also in Finland and London too, and are still in touch. It is always thrilling when God answers prayers in an unexpected way, but also a thrill when God uses one to answer someone else's prayer. "I, being in the way, the Lord led me."

More flowers on the table

Tim was very young, 18 perhaps? He was tall and boyish and had come to join us camping on a Purpose Holiday. We all loved him as we got to know him. He gave his everything to camp life, washed up with no complaints and helped everywhere when a bit of extra strength was needed. There wasn't much finery around the camp. Everything was pretty basic, and rough and dusty. Surprises often spring out of nowhere and this was a big one for me. Somewhere I'd found some wild flowers and a jar of some sort and put them on our table. Tim was ecstatic. Tim went on to be a missionary in India, married a French wife and is now pioneering ways of sharing the gospel in France.

Canoeing

Our adventures with Purpose Holidays have meant we have spent a least 4 years of our lives living in our caravan. On our way to the holiday resorts on the coast of the Mediterranean we were able to visit cities and places of huge interest. We have loved the simple and outdoor life and got quite adept at setting up camp and somehow being comfortable in unexpected places. Having been in resorts all summer, we chose to take our own holidays coming slowly home enjoying the country we were passing through.

One thing we discovered was canoeing. The general arrangement is that you hire a canoe and get dropped into the river at that point. Then you canoe down the river for several hours to a certain rendezvous point where you are met and taken back to base by minibus. You are provided with 2 paddles and a small barrel with a screw-on lid, in which you can put your pullovers and valuables. You take your own picnic. It is a good lesson in teamwork, and who is boss. You learn what works and what doesn't, and that you have to do certain things in different ways in different situations.

A doddle

The first river we tackled was the Dordogne, a lovely river that winds its way between the castles of the English and French during the Hundred Years War. Unexpectedly, the English castles are on the south bank and the French ones on the north bank. This is all because Eleanor of Aquitaine had married Henry II of England. Every now and again, the river speeds up over 'ripples', which are quite exciting for beginners. The secret is to paddle hard in order to keep straight on. Otherwise you are in danger of going round in circles, and possibly capsizing.

Next we graduated to the Tarn, which is definitely a grade up, faster flowing with some real rapids. We reckoned we were definitely getting the idea and acquiring some proficiency, having successfully negotiated all hazards without coming out. We gave ourselves a metaphorical pat on the back.

A real challenge

With these skills under our belts our next objective was the Ardèche, a much faster flowing river. It ran for 16½ miles through a 1,000 foot deep gorge. There was one telephone point halfway along where one could request rescue by helicopter. Once in the river there was no turning back for 6 hours plus stops. We had bought a map of the river. This showed which side of major rocks and rapids to aim for if the river was running high or if it was running low, but on our day it was somewhere in between, so we had to make our own decisions.

At the beginning of the day we met a couple of ladies (not quite young) in a kayak, who seemed to have no map, and so would like to look at ours. There was a photographer just beside the first rapid producing photographs for sale at the end of the journey. One couldn't of course resist buying a copy. We paddled furiously through this first rapid which was much more sportive than anything we had met on the Tarn, and we have the photo to prove it, see page 94.

After passing a canoe bent into an L shape, what happened at the second major rapid, we don't know. The canoe overturned and we came out. It may have been some confusion of command, or we thought we should do one thing but did the opposite. We were in the fast flowing river desperately hanging on to our paddles. That is the golden rule, as without them one is helpless. The canoe, with the water-tight barrel tied to one of the seats, was rescued by the swarm of young boys who were there every day to watch the exciting spectacle of adults capsizing. I found myself on the left bank under the cliff. David landed on the right bank, where further down the boys had beached the canoe. I knew what he would do, he would shout across the river, "Swim." There was in fact no alternative. So I had to swim up river with my paddle, against the fast flowing current, so as to hopefully land on the other side somewhere near him. In the end we only lost one plastic shoe between us. We took a deep breath and a pause to regain our composure, and set off again.

The two ladies in the kayak were bumping along unperturbed, and, as complete beginners, never came out at all. We managed the rest of the journey without capsizing again, and enjoyed it hugely. At one place we had to pull our canoe over some shingle, only to find ourselves in the middle of a nudist camp and being graciously helped by a man dressed only in a hat.

Wet, wounded and happy

At the end of the 16½ miles, over six hours later we paddled the last straight stretch out of the gorge. A man on the bank shouted across to us, "Vous êtes très vieux." I replied, "Non monsieur, nous sommes très mouillés." - not very old, but very wet!

The evening sun shone and the photographer was there to sell his picture of us, which we continue to display with pride. I tried to get out of the canoe, but found I couldn't put my foot to the ground. Later a doctor we visited asked if I had hit it or twisted it. I said I had no idea, as I was underneath the canoe. It was a new experience for me to travel home for the next few days, hopping up and down the caravan step on crutches. They have a special place in the corner of our garage and have come in useful on several subsequent occasions.

My audacious father

My father was more of a businessman than a farmer, quite a loner, which acted against him among his fellow farmers. Perhaps this was a result of hard experiences in both world wars. One of his qualities was a certain audacity, which may have accounted for his successes. One example I always enjoyed hearing about, was when he was in the army in the Second World War. He was marching his troop down Reigate Hill, when they passed a tea party on the lawn of a house close to the road. He sent his troop on, in charge of the sergeant, and made a detour up the drive of this house. Introducing himself, he said, "Your tea party looked so nice I felt I must come and join you." They were delighted and quickly made space for him to join them, which resulted in an ongoing friendship.

When the burden of worry that I carried rolled off my shoulders when I became a Christian, perhaps some of his audacity was allowed to come through. His spirit of adventure has certainly stood me in good stead, as I have found myself living in Africa, camping for months at a time in Europe, and latterly living in many Russian cities in fairly primitive and surprising conditions.

Cancer

When, after eight years, David was made redundant by Intercon in 1981, because they had a financial shortfall which caused them to close down part of their ministry, we thought we might be able to buy the flat in Bolton Gardens in which we had lived for 17 years and which had been provided for us by both our employers, but we couldn't. So we moved out of London to Basingstoke.

Just before the move, I became a little suspicious that I might have something wrong. No one likes to think of cancer, and in spite of the many advances in medical science it is still a major illness. The doctor I saw couldn't find anything wrong and suggested I register with a doctor in Basingstoke and get checked again on arrival there. This I did. This second doctor was also unable to find anything wrong. Reassured by two doctors, I thought there couldn't be anything wrong, so I put it behind me and concentrated on our 2 to 3 month long visits working in Europe from our second-hand caravan. However while we were on our second such summer journey I was feeling some discomfort. So on arriving home, I returned to the doctor, who immediately made an appointment for me to see the hospital surgeon.

David in the meantime had to do a quick turn around and, complete with a tent and sleeping bag, fly out to Ibiza to prepare for and meet one of our Purpose Holiday teams arriving there shortly. He was unobtainable for the rest of the week. He had left me instructions to plan something for our silver wedding with our new neighbours, and our family and friends. We thought a croquet party would be appropriate. I had a biopsy and a second appointment with a cancer specialist. I drove myself to the hospital and was told I needed a mastectomy as I did have cancer after all! What do you say on receiving that kind of information? I remember asking when the operation would be, and was told the lists were closed for that week, but that I should be admitted in two weeks time. "It's not very nice to tell a lady that," he said. I thanked him for his kindness and drove home!

I remember thinking there were some things to talk about with your husband first, and that this was one of them. But he was in Ibiza and I couldn't reach him. I didn't want to talk to friends or family before talking to him, so I prayed and planned to get on with sending out silver wedding invitations and weeding the garden, etc. I felt perfectly peaceful, but now the questions began to come into my mind. But, as I asked them, each one was met by what I was reading in the Bible that day.

Who has a croquet set?

When David returned from abroad, we went to my doctor together to find out if a mastectomy was the only treatment available. We were reassured by her that in my case it was definitely the best answer. I asked her how long I would need to be in hospital because we were planning our silver wedding croquet party. Then I found myself telling her that we didn't have a croquet set, and did she by any chance have one? I had only seen her twice and didn't know her, and I was horrified by my audacity. "Yes" she said, "I do have one and I'll send my boys round with it this afternoon." Filled with embarrassment, we left.

True to her word, her two sons of 17 and 19, who were both at Winchester College, arrived with the croquet set and, over orange squash in the garden, we discovered that they had become Christians at school through a helpful master, and that their mother had also just found Christ herself.

Encouragements

Before the 'op' we asked our local church if they would pray for me, and the two churchwardens came round to pray with us. One of them left me with the song, "Father I place into your hands the things I can't do." We also asked friends to pray, so two couples came round the evening before I went into hospital and three out of the four of them said they wanted to read a particular Scripture passage without having consulted each other. All three came up with the very same passage, 'Fear not, and be not dismayed....for the battle is not yours but God's.' 2 Chronicles 20:15.

With these encouragements I went into hospital. I believed the Lord could heal the cancer if he wanted to. Or, I thought, it would be fun if the surgeon operated and just found a hole where the cancer had been. Or maybe there were good reasons in God's plan why I should have cancer and this operation in this hospital at this particular time.

During the first day's preliminaries and preparations, I remember going over to another woman's bed and sharing our evening hot chocolate together. She had spent some years in Kenya and we had much in common. She was full of anxiety, as she had emphysema through smoking and even after it was diagnosed she wasn't told that she shouldn't smoke!

There was a lovely ward sister who was kindness itself and always seemed to be there at the most important moments, taking stitches out herself, and when you had your first bath, etc. She was also very sceptical about there being a loving God because she had seen so much suffering.

In a cancer ward

When I went into hospital to have the operation, I felt "Now I really am ill," and so I could settle down into my own cocoon, read my book and keep myself to myself. But I knew as a Christian with good news to share I couldn't do that. By now we were about five in the ward. My Kenyan friend was so anxious that I prayed, "Lord if there is a time when she doesn't have any visitors and I don't either, I'll go and share what you've done for us." And one day that opportunity came.

I taught all in the ward the song that I had been given: "Father I place into your hands...." and we would sing it together. One evening the young house doctor came running down the passage saying, "What's all this noise about?" "O, we're just singing" I said, "We'll sing it for you too."

Our silver wedding

We had our silver wedding while I was in hospital, and we felt we wanted to tell the young disillusioned nurses that marriage was all right. I asked David to bring in a cake so everyone could have a piece from the cleaner to the consultant and everyone's visitors. Someone sent me a beautiful bouquet of flowers so I took the ribbon off it and bounded it all round my cubicle rail so as to greet David when he came in. Everyone knew it was our silver wedding day.

When the drugs trolley arrived in the evening, it seemed to be accompanied by many more people than usual. We found there weren't drugs on the trolley but another cake made especially in the hospital kitchen, and champagne provided for everyone. There was the surgeon and the house doctor and everyone, celebrating with us. The message of that day was "marriage is okay."

The next day was the Croquet Party Day. The tubes were tucked away under my dress and I was allowed out for the day. So the croquet party went ahead with fun and games. Our guests kindly produced the food. It was a huge success. When everyone had gone, David and I opened cards and good wishes and he eventually took me back to the hospital at 9pm. They apparently thought I had left for good and wasn't ever coming back!

Allowed out of hospital for the day

Needy people

Following my mastectomy operation, it was found that the cancer was not contained so I needed radiotherapy. Netley Abbey, a big house which belonged to the NHS, was to be my home for five days a week for six weeks. I could return home at weekends. About 40 of us were based there and were bussed into Southampton General Hospital each day. The treatment only took a few minutes, but we had to don Paisley patterned dressing gowns and wait our turn. I remember being surprised that people were so nervous that if they left the room to get a cup of coffee they would miss their turn. So I made it my business to collect their money and take coffee to them each day. They needed it.

I remember feeling very lonely when I first arrived at Netley Abbey. I went for a walk along the path by Southampton Water, wondering if I would ever get to know my fellow patients, let alone encourage them or be able to tell them that God loved them. They all looked quite composed, but of course they weren't underneath. I remember passing some blackberry bushes and eating some, and suddenly realising that just as the fruit was under the leaves, it was only as I got to know people that I would discover what their needs were. That night I remember talking to a lady from the Isle of Wight and heard her say, "You can live for years without giving God a thought, until something like this happens to you."

I was struggling with some knitting one night and the nurse on duty and I were joking. She said she thought I'd better undo the whole thing and start again. Then suddenly she said, "Mrs Steele, I would like to know what makes you tick?" You never know what people are going to see in your life, and which ones want to find out what it's all about.

Radiotherapy opportunities

There were no mobile phones in those days and everyone had to use the limited number of house phones in the evenings, so I found I could call David more conveniently after breakfast. One morning after speaking to him, I found my watch had stopped, and that I'd missed both the ambulances that took us to the hospital. Thinking I should probably have to take a taxi, I went downstairs and found to my relief that they were calling a third ambulance that morning as there were more of us than usual. I was much later than usual to the hospital that morning and assigned to a different waiting area.

Each morning there were lots of people who came by day from further afield. Among them was a man who always seemed smiling and joking. This particular morning I found myself sitting next to him and somehow got talking to him about how I had found God. He asked me if knowing God helps in this situation, and listened intently as I told him that it did. "You do wonder, don't you", he said. I would never have had the opportunity to talk with him alone if my watch hadn't stopped that morning.

Winchester

After five years in Basingstoke our lives moved on to Winchester. We needed a house with an office for David away from the main living area. In Worthy Park Grove we found the perfect place, a house built for a retired couple with an extra room beyond the kitchen for David's office. There was more garden than we had before, but we thought we could manage it.

We had possession of the house before moving in, so with a picnic table and a kettle we were doing some preparatory jobs. We needed to board the loft, so David had arranged for sheets of 8 x 4 chipboard to be delivered. I was weeding the drive in front of the house and feeling slightly overwhelmed, and wondering if we had done the right thing.

The lorry with the boards arrived and David and the driver started getting it up into the loft. Soon there was a call for tea and we met around the picnic table for a pause in their heavy work. I don't remember the driver's name, but he was soon telling us how he and his wife had very recently returned from a year in Australia. They had led pretty wild lives out there but had found Jesus Christ who had turned their lives around, and the change was affecting their extended family. We were eventually able to say, "We are Christians too." "Yes, I know," he said. We don't to this day know how he knew. With our new found friend we prayed for each other.

To earn some money quickly, he was on his first day working for a builders' merchant. His first assignment was to deliver this boarding to us, to his and our encouragement as we shared and prayed together.

My doubts about our move evaporated. This meeting was more than a coincidence. I was sure we were meant to be here and that the years would reveal the rightness of the move.

A new kitchen and the salesman

We took over a very impractical kitchen with very little work-top space and only a few cupboards and appliances that were about to die. We needed to replace and modernise. We planned to move the few existing kitchen cupboards to the utility room and start again in the kitchen with something that would be not too different. The hunt was on and eventually I found a near match in Homebase. I had taken a drawer of the old units with me in my search, but I wanted to be sure by taking a piece of the new units back to our kitchen to double check.

I asked the salesman if this would be possible. He was very unsure and said he couldn't check with anyone, because his boss was on holiday. I promised I would only take a small drawer one night at 7pm, just before they closed, and return it exactly when they opened at 9am the next morning, so only the mice would miss it. I said that if we chose those particular units I would give him a box of Smarties. He was reluctantly persuaded, but admitted the next day when I re-turned the small drawer, that he had spent a sleepless night thinking I wouldn't come back and that he would probably lose his job.

The carpenter and the storm

We knew we would need help with the kitchen so phoned Ken, an expert carpenter who had helped us with some re-cladding of our house in Basingstoke with a great eye for detail. He agreed to do it, as he liked to take on one kitchen a year. David had planned it in great detail, exactly where everything was to go. The day came to get started. Ken arrived and as the first morning progressed, so did the wind howling around the house.

We had been abroad when the great summer storm of 1987 struck Britain, so didn't immediately realised the signs of another. I was slightly surprised when branches started falling off the trees at the front of the house. One brought down the electricity supply cable at 11am so we had no light and no heat. It was 25 January 1990. Then as the storm raged, at 12 noon there was a great thud - the 90 foot Scots Pine at the bottom of the garden was lying across the lawn. Other trees were falling too.

"How am I going to work my electric tools?" says Ken, "It will be hand tools."…. "We'll help you, and when you absolutely need the electricity for something it'll come on. The Lord is our helper," we replied. We found our camping Gaz stove for making hot soup and tea. My job was to hold torches so Ken and David could see, and hold screws, etc, and make picnic meals and do anything else needed. We found the units were flat packed and needed assembling, so that was David's first job. So we became team 'A'.

Great fun

It all became the greatest fun as we worked away together. Every so often there would be a shout from David, "Stop, this isn't going to work." Or from Ken, "Stop, this isn't going to work." We would all gather round and work out a revised plan, and on we would go.

Each day before Ken left for his home in Basingstoke and his wife's hot meal waiting for him, he would say, "Dave before I come in the morning, you might like to do such and such, and Shirl, you might like to do another thing," and off he would go.

We were left in a cold house with no hot water and only one tiny Camping Gaz ring to heat up some soup, and candles to see by. Exhausted but happy, we would fill hot water bottles and fall into bed until Ken arrived at 8am the next morning. This went on for almost a whole week. Every day we would greet him with "Ebenezer," which means 'Hitherto hath the Lord helped us'. "Well, yes he has," he would say.

Then came the day when Ken pronounced, "Tomorrow I must use my electric tools to cut holes out of the worktop for the sink and the hob." At six o'clock that night the electricity came on, and the next day he could use his power tools.

One of the innovations we specially wanted to incorporate was a 2-shelf Finnish draining cupboard above the sink. We had the plastic-coated wire shelves that we had brought from Finland, and Ken cut out the bottom of the cupboard so we could fit them in. Ken's two sons also helped briefly, to fix the hob and the sink, one an electrician and the other a plumber.

Helpful Hints

Work clean in the kitchen.

Keeping a kitchen under some sort of control and in some sort of order, so that one knows roughly where one is and where one is going to, needs some hints to achieve it. My six hints would be:

1. Put newspaper in the bottom of your refuse bin inside the plastic liner. You can fold several in a spare moment, and keep them on one side. This helps to absorb moisture, so that you don't carry dripping bags to the wheely bin.

2. If you have a tile or vinyl floor, have a mat where you stand at the sink. This will take drips so you aren't walking on them or slipping on them. The floor will keep clean too, and it will be softer for your feet.

3. Never put a dirty spoon directly onto the work-top. Always put it on a plate or saucer. This is easily moved and your work-top remains clean for the next job.

4. Always keep a moist J-cloth handy to wipe away spills or crumbs or vegetable shavings as they occur, so the work top is free for the next job.

5. Sort washing up before you start doing it, i.e. plates together, cups together. Order is satisfying.

6. Keep a plastic jug by the sink specifically for receiving soiled cutlery to soak. Fill it 1/3rd with water. It makes washing up cutlery much easier, and also helps to keep the work-top tidy and clean.

The kitchen opening party

We reckoned that to complete the project we must have a 'Kitchen Opening Party' while our Finnish friends were with us. We planned to invite everyone involved to 'coffee and dessert', including their husbands and wives or girlfriends.

Ken cut the ribbon across the kitchen door, so we could all go in to view it. And Nalle cut the ribbon across the Finnish cupboard and she and her friend sang Finnish songs. The guests had come at 8pm but it was still going on at 11pm. Several felt slightly amazed that they could enjoy a party so much with no alcohol.

Best of all, the salesman from Homebase got his box of Smarties and had no idea how to react. Team 'A' had succeeded, and the smiles and memories remain, let alone the enjoyment of such a special kitchen. For us it was an experience of 'Our Father in heaven being interested in us constructing our kitchen'.

Intercepted

Pirkko had phoned from Portugal. Her aunt had died and she was now head of the family and must return to Finland for the funeral. She would come via England and spend the night with us en route. She gave us the time of her plane's arrival at Gatwick. With David having planned the route I should take, off I set to drive to meet her. Ten minutes after leaving, David received a phone call from Pirkko. She had missed her plane and was re-routed to Heathrow! These were the days before mobile phones. David, wondering how he could contact me, tried to think if he knew any vicars on the route that he had worked out for me. Perhaps one of them could waylay me and I could be diverted to Heathrow instead of going all the way to Gatwick?

As he thought about it and prayed, he remembered Sara who had been an air hostess and was living in Guildford. He thought she might be willing to try to find me as I would soon be coming off the Hog's Back and down the Guildford bypass. When he phoned her, he found that her husband David Thompson was on the last day of a three-month sabbatical and at that moment papering his hall. Hearing the story he eagerly agreed to try to locate me and give me new directions to Heathrow. He jumped into his red sports car and drove to the Guildford bypass. Just as he came to the end of his road he saw our blue Renault passing in front of him. The chase began.

Skilfully manoeuvring in front of me, he starts attracting my attention and waving to me to follow him off on the next slip road. I recognize him and think, "It must be his lunch hour", quite forgetting that he worked in London. "How very kind of him to wave me behind him," I thought, "but I'm going to meet my friend at Gatwick so I can't stop! I shall have to ring him tonight and tell him why", so on I went.

However my David had warned him that I was on a single-minded mission and would be hard to stop. So he gets back on to the route David has told him I'll be taking and tries to catch up with me again. By now I've turned off the bypass towards Gatwick.

Suddenly, there he is again in front of me and waving to me again! "How extraordinary" I thought, "I really can't be rude to him a second time, I shall have to pull in and just say a brief hello". So he gets out of his car and comes to my window and says, "I've got a message from David for you", so we head back to his house for a cup of tea and I phone my David to re-route me to Heathrow to meet Pirkko.

As she's missed the original flight, I have plenty of time to get to Heathrow before she does. As soon as we meet, Pirkko is full of apologies. "Don't worry", I say, "I've had an amazing experience."

Pirkko's story

On the way home Pirkko tells me her side of the story. Hearing of her aunt's death she plans her journey back to Finland and arranges for her time away from Portugal. The travel agent mentions two departure times. When Pirkko arrives at the airport thinking she is in good time, she finds the plane has already left. And she has no redress. She asks the girl at the counter what she should do, and is told there is nothing she can do. At that moment an official looking lady comes up and asks if she can help. Pirkko tells her the story of her need, that she has missed the plane to get her to her aunt's funeral. "Come with me" she says, and then asks Pirkko to sit and wait. In the East when someone asked for directions, the usual answer would be, "I am the way, come with me." Jesus, giving directions for our lives says, "I am the Way, come with me."

Pirkko, now being head of the family, must be the one to make a speech at her aunt's funeral. She hasn't had a moment to think about it, so she gets out her notebook and starts getting her thoughts together and putting them on paper. Half an hour later the lady returns and tells her she is now booked on the next plane, to Heathrow. "How much does it cost?" says Pirkko. "There is nothing to pay," says her rescuer. Pirkko expected to have to buy a new ticket to pay for her mistake of misunderstanding the time, but found her new ticket was a free gift. There was nothing to pay.

As we asked for God's help that day, he stepped in to answer David's prayer and Pirkko's prayers too, and there was much thanksgiving and excitement, as we saw and heard the drama of that day worked out, not only in our household, but in the highwayman's household too.

Verbier

After being chaplain many times in Zermatt, we were asked to transfer and help chaplains make the most of the new opportunities in Verbier. An English entrepreneur, who owned an apartment in Verbier, had become a Christian and was driving 1½ hours to services in Vevey. 'With so many British visiting Verbier', he thought, 'There ought to be English services in Verbier'.

One Sunday he met the chairman of Intercon and suggested his idea. The chairman said that if he would provide accommodation for the chaplains, Intercon would make all the other arrangements. That was the start of the English services in the Swiss Protestant chapel on Sunday evenings at 6pm, ski-ing chaplains going fortnightly throughout each winter season.

After three years, with other calls on their resources, Intercon handed over to David the whole responsibility for this enterprise. It still has its twofold purpose: to help and to reach out to English-speaking skiers and to provide half holiday and half ministry opportunities for skiing chaplains.

This has continued for the last 19 years. During this time we've had six different apartments to operate from. Each apartment in its different way has provided a base and a warm venue for hospitality, with open house for tea once a week and many people sharing meals with the chaplains and their wives. The chaplains also have many opportunities to meet people on the slopes, in the lifts and buses, in the restaurants, shops and bars, in the tour operator's chalets and at Ski Club parties.

There have been many opportunities to encourage people. I recall a girl, who met David in the sauna; she expressed a wish to find God. He suggested she came to meet me in the apartment, and could I perhaps lend her a book? She came and we talked for a long time, and we have met many times since.

Another opportunity was meeting up with a chalet girl whose mother had come to the church. It was the beginning of a life changing experience for her and we are still in touch. She later told us that she came to Verbier to find God.

One New Years Eve we had a call from someone we had known superficially for many years. She was desperate,

"Finding Nemmo"

In England a friend of ours enthusiastically told me that although "Finding Nemmo" was a children's film, it was so delightful that one should see it. On our next visit to Verbier I noticed "Finding Nemmo" was on at the local cinema and so one afternoon, when David was busy, I went to see it. As I stood waiting to buy a ticket a large Red Setter dog pressed himself against me, which made me exclaim out loud, "I think I have to buy two tickets because this dog seems to be coming in with me". There was a lady with a six-year-old boy standing near and we laughed and started talking. I went into the cinema with them and sat just behind them.

When the film was over we enthused together as we came out. She then turned to me and asked if I would have a cup of coffee with them. I learned she was from Serbia and was married to a Swiss. We exchanged telephone numbers and agreed to meet again.

As she gained confidence she began to tell me of the difficulties in her marriage. Over a period of two or more years we've been able to meet in Verbier from time to time, so I've been able to keep in touch and pray for her and encourage her, and I'm glad to say the family is now back together again. As I pray for God's leading each day, I believe it was more than chance that a big Red Setter pressed himself against my side and my exclamation started a conversation with this young mother.

Christmas and Easter services bring many to the little chapel who normally never go to church. They hear the truth about God put in a relevant way.

The Royal Armoured Corps training scheme brings out many, some of whom are just about to go to Iraq or Afghanistan, or have just come back from those battle zones. Life and death issues are very much on their minds, and the army carol service gives each of them an opportunity to hear from a chaplain the relevance of Jesus Christ's life and death for every individual.

The English chaplaincy is very much part of the scene in Verbier now. We met an hotelier in the street there one early December who said, "Now the chaplain has arrived, the season can begin."

Chivalry shown by a small boy

Returning home from Switzerland once, we made a detour via Eton to deliver something to friends. Being so near to Windsor Castle and not having seen the restored St.George's Hall since the fire there, we thought we'd cross the river and find out if the castle was open. Finding it shut, we made for one of those delightful cafes on the pavement in a small side street nearby so as to have a cup of tea.

As we sat at a table, a family came past, father, mother and their son of about seven. Recently I had needed to have a small lump removed from the bridge of my nose and had a plaster across it. The young boy dressed as a knight in armour, complete with rubber sword, passed us but then returned and said, "I do hope you'll soon be better." So I thanked him. Whereupon he explained, "It's called a patch," and then went on his way to rejoin his parents. The days of chivalry are not over.

Grandchildren

Often when we return from a journey away somewhere, we do a big shop at a local supermarket before arriving home. On this occasion it was mid-morning so I suggested we might drop in at the new Winchester service station, which we had never seen, and have a cup of coffee before doing the shopping. There we discovered an attractive cafe area and had our coffee. David then left me to finish mine, while he went to look at the maps. At the next table there was a family, an older lady with grey hair with an older man and three boys about 10, 8 and 6. They were all poring over some puzzle they were concentrating on together.

If you don't happen to have any children, the downside is that you can't have any grandchildren, and I find I miss them dreadfully and go quite potty over little people that I pass in the street or find myself watching.

Seeing this lovely family interacting together struck a chord in me and I found myself starting to cry. "Oh Lord you know," I said as the tears trickled down my cheeks. As quick as lightning the answer came back "I didn't have any grandchildren either." "Nor you did" I thought, "you completely understand." David had left me sitting there completely happy but came back to find me in floods of tears. But tears of awe and wonder and gratitude that my heavenly Father completely understood.

Helpful Hints

Ladies

I don't know about you, but I have noticed that some of us ladies of a certain age upwards (we look with envy at those who don't have a problem and seem to remain pencil thin) become aware that our waistbands are a little tight! We aren't getting fat exactly and the scales aren't ringing alarm bells, but we feel slightly tummyish and somehow don't want to put on certain blouses or slacks any more. That is rather awkward because we like them and they go with other things!

Look up, all is not lost! The secret is the longer line. We must now wear blouses outside rather than tucked in. This isn't quite as simple as it sounds because the blouse hems need to be shortened with a slit made at each side to be comfortable and look good. For those who are 'needle happy' this won't be a problem. But for those who aren't it might be worth finding a helpful dressmaker. Get her to turn all your blouses into neat tops that lengthen your waistline and subtly cover those naughty and unsightly rings!

2 Ukranian and 18 Russian cities where Shirley and David have given leadership training

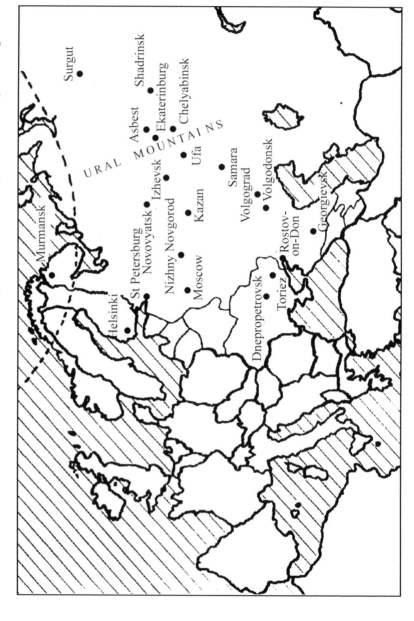

URAL MOUNTAINS

Surgut

Shadrinsk

Asbest

Ekaterinburg

Chelyabinsk

Ufa

Samara

Volgodonsk

Volgograd

Izhevsk

Kazan

Georgievsk

St Petersburg

Novovyatsk

Nizhny Novgorod

Rostov-on-Don

Moscow

Toriez

Murmansk

Dnepropetrovsk

Helsinki

Russia opens up
Babushka - v - Cossacks

The English team, of which we were a part, had been sent in October 1992 to help prepare Rostov-on-Don, a city of a million people, for 'Mission Volga'. In small groups, we had spoken at universities and schools and other institutes. Now we awaited the ship carrying Kalevi Lehtinen and his team to start the mission in the stadium. It was due to arrive around 7pm. It was a dark and slightly drizzly evening as we stood on the quayside.

The Cossacks are the military wing of the Orthodox Church to counter attacks by other faiths. Somehow they had been told that their old enemy the Turks were coming, so they were there looking rather sinister with their sabres, and determined that the group on the ship was not going to land in their city. Also waiting for the ship's arrival was a grandmother or babushka. She had prayed for three years that God would do something for her city and now the Christians were coming. She was there to welcome them with a beautifully crocheted white tablecloth to put down in the mud for the first Christians to step out on. The Cossacks obviously didn't want her there and she wasn't going to move. The police weren't too sure how to proceed.

Our leader advised that the police allow the Cossacks to make their demonstration. This they did and then melted away in the darkness. So the babushka achieved her dream and Kalevi's team were able to disembark to a great welcome.

Visiting the Metropolitan

Six months later we were in Rostov again, this time to help the churches with follow up of the mission. David arranged to pay a courtesy call on the new Metropolitan to offer aid. The rouble had just been greatly devalued. He arrived with his interpreter into a sea of variously robed Orthodox monks and priests. He told me later that he felt like an American in the court of King Arthur.

After half an hour David's interpreter learnt that she needed to catch the sleeve of the metropolitan's secretary as he flew through. Not knowing what he looked like or how he was dressed didn't help. After a while he was pointed out and she caught the hem of his garment. In his office he told us of the atrocities perpetrated by the Nazis as they passed through his Ukrainian home town twice when he was a boy, on their way to and from Stalingrad, now renamed Volgograd.

After another half hour the diminutive Metropolitan Vladimir appeared and ushered them into his palatial office. His English was almost perfect because he had hired an English teacher when he represented the Orthodox Church at the World Council of Churches in Geneva during the Soviet era and had then listened regularly and clandestinely to the BBC News ever since. When David, referring to humanitarian and financial aid said, "How can we help you?" Vladimir thought for a while and then surprisingly replied,

"When my priests and people say to me, 'What shall we do?' I say to them, 'Remember Moses and the people of Israel in the wilderness. God provided daily food and their shoes didn't wear out. Rostov-on-Don is not as bad as the wilderness.' Please pray for us." He has since been Metropolitan of St. Petersburg.

Chelyabinsk in West Siberia

Alina was our interpreter in Chelyabinsk. She had a small son of six and lived with her atheist mother and father. The greatest excitement for her son on a public holiday was a walk in the park with his mother. Alina did all she could to help her son to know the truth of the Bible, and sometimes found children's videos to help him. His grandfather used to love to watch these videos with his grandson and began to learn from them himself.

As grandmother watched these sessions, she decided to put Jesus to the test to see if he was really alive or not? She decided she would ask him for a specific kitten. It must be a blue Persian kitten. Not long after, she was uncharacteristically sitting outside her block of flats on a bench when a small girl came running up to her saying, "Please, please would you look after this little cat, it's going to die." It was a blue Persian kitten and Alina's mother took it in much to her grandson's delight.

But she decided it just might be a coincidence that the kitten happened to be a blue Persian kitten, so she would test Jesus again. "Jesus," she said, "I want a dog with very small legs, and very short hair." The very next day she was walking to her local shop and at the crossroads there was quite a commotion going on. Someone was saying, "Please someone rescue that little dog, because it's going to get run over." It was a little dog with very short legs and very short hair and Alina's mother took it home. Later that week a girl knocked on her door with a dog in her arms saying, "Please could you look after this little dog?" It had very short legs and very short hair. Alina told us that her mother threw up her hands and exclaimed, "Jesus, it's enough, it's enough!"

We knew that Alina's family was very poor and sometimes couldn't buy food. The granny used to cook for the little boy, but sometimes Alina and her father would come home to tea and biscuits only. So we were wondering how they fed the kitten and the little dog. They told us that a Jewish family came to them from time to time with a bucket of scraps from their table.

Alina learnt early to tell God her needs, disappointments and troubles. One day when she was praying and telling God about her particular troubles, she stopped and said, "Dear God, I'm always telling you my troubles, what are your troubles?" Immediately, the answer came, "Rwanda." Next time we saw her a year later she asked us, "What is Rwanda?" She had never heard the word and had no idea that it was a country where a terrible genocide was happening at that time. How many of us have ever asked God what his troubles are?

On our return to England we told Ken Barham, formerly a bishop in Rwanda, who told his colleagues out there. They were amazed and greatly heartened that God cared so much that he told a Christian in Siberia that his chief trouble at that time was the situation in their small country thousands of miles away in Africa.

Arctic Murmansk

Murmansk was a name I had known of for many years. In my late teens, I had had a boyfriend who was a sailor on the convoys which took supplies to the Russians during the war around Norway's North Cape, well north of the Arctic Circle. This was possible even in midwinter because of the warmth of the Gulf Stream preventing the sea there from freezing over. I still have a bracelet of Russian kopecks on a chain, which he brought me.

The Baptist church there had asked us to give training to group leaders, so we went 36 hours by train north of St Petersburg. In the corridor there was a printed list of the 99 scheduled stops. What we also didn't expect was to find was a metre of permafrost, which stays all year round. And it was May with snow driving in horizontally on a biting east wind. Mounds of snow still covered buried cars, and we needed every bit of warm clothing we could lay our hands on.

The church was welcoming and the course was enthusiastically accepted. David's interpreter, Victor was in the Merchant Navy and spoke excellent English. He was planning a short holiday in St Petersburg, so we invited him to be our travelling companion on the return journey. Many people were travelling south at that time, wanting a change of scene and some warmth. Train tickets were in such demand that church people started queueing for us at about 5am.

Because of the crowds, we knew we'd have a fourth companion in our compartment, where the seats would become bunks at night for the 36-hour journey south. We began to pray with Victor about who this would be at such close quarters with us for all those hours. We boarded the train shortly after midnight to find a quiet looking young man about Victor's age already installed. Soon we were to settle down for the night, so Victor and this other man withdrew to the corridor, while David and I made up our bunks and put on our tracksuits. Then we went out into the corridor while they did the same. When we returned to the compartment, Victor introduced Valodia, and told us that he had once met a Canadian missionary and had lots of questions. As it was now after 2am and we would have a whole day and another night together, we thought that the questions could wait till morning.

Each carriage on a Russian train has a 'Provotnik'. She has special charge of her passengers to make sure they re-board the train in time after stops. She adds coal and stokes the boiler at the end of the carriage to make sure the samovar is always ready to provide boiling water for tea, which she will sometimes bring you. She can look very fierce, but usually has the heart of a sheepdog.

When morning came, we reversed the process of the night before. Then the four of us pooled the food which we had brought with us for breakfast and began to get to know each other. I had wondered what book Volodia had been reading. It turned out to be a Bible. He was second-in-command of a Russian nuclear submarine based in the military zone just north of Murmansk and he was a navigator, the same as Victor was in the Merchant Navy. He had just become a Christian but was very confused, and with many questions to ask. So here we were, David with much biblical study under his belt and Victor the perfect interpreter.

So for many hours Volodia's questions got answered, and his smile got bigger and bigger and our friendship and fellowship got deeper. Sometimes when people hear of a long 99-stop 36-hour journey on a Russian train, they say, "How awful." But to us it was sweet and not long enough, and we didn't want it to end. Volodia was coming south to look for somewhere to take his wife and child on holiday.

On arrival in St Petersburg, we were met at our carriage by a Russian friend who had come to meet us in his car. Our travelling companions could have left us there, but no, they had to come with us all the way across the station and to the other side of the road, where our friend's car was parked. Only then did we reluctantly part and go our separate ways. It's not been possible to keep in touch, but one day in heaven we will rejoice as we remember those 36 hours together, where we had no telephone, or radio, or television to distract us from God's purpose: to answer Volodia's questions and help him on his Christian journey.

Ekaterinburg

We were in Ekaterinburg, invited by the Baptist church to give training for leaders of small Bible discussion groups. They had some rooms in the basement of a block of flats. I had quite a mixed group of ladies, and there was an assortment of benches and chairs. We managed to form somewhat of a circle and got started.

On one of the seven evenings we were with them water started coming through the ceiling. Soon buckets were found to catch what was falling from above. Eventually we discovered that earlier that day the water had been turned off, and probably the people upstairs had tried to turn on a tap but got no water, and then went out forgetting to turn the tap off. So when the water came on again in the evening their sink filled up and went on overflowing down to us in the basement. We had to change our seating positions and work around the buckets. So it was even more difficult to maintain the circle. No one expressed any frustration; everyone simply accepted the situation. It had no doubt happened before and would probably happen again. Russians are patient people, dealing with similar situations on a daily basis.

The main purpose of the training is to help people apply God's word to their lives. It is a difficult concept for Russians who are very much ideas people and love to discuss. At the end of each discussion we try to help people to apply something that they have discovered. Ideally it should be personal, possible, practical and measurable. It's not helpful to say, "I'm going to read the whole Old Testament this week," With all else that needs doing, it's not possible.

A retired history Professor, called Martha, when it came to sharing her application, said she was going to do many extra things before tomorrow evening! I tried to explain that if you wanted to move a pile of bricks from one point to another, you would take one brick and move it, and then another and another, so in the end all the bricks would be moved over. That's why we were thinking of trying to apply one thing at a time. "But," she said, "in Russia, we would pick up the whole pile of bricks and move them all together." I tried again. "Shirley," she said, "Are you going to take on the whole Soviet Union?" "Yes," I said.

An emergency en route to Ukraine

We had been leading some courses in Asbest in 1998 and were on our way to do the same for the second time in Ukraine. We booked with Donaire, one of the 300 Baby-flots that Aeroflot split into soon after the Soviet Union collapsed. We understood that the 2½ hour flight from Ekaterinburg to Rostov-on-Don was direct. So we were surprised when in only 45 minutes the plane came down rather steeply in Ufa. The air hostess had seemed somewhat disorganised in distributing the usual cups of water and pieces of bread to us all. But this was Russia, and we couldn't understand the announcements coming over the PA. On landing we saw fire engines waiting. Eventually we found the Intourist Office where someone spoke English. "Oh," she said, "we were very worried, you made an emergency landing. You weren't supposed to land here at all. The plane has a fault. We don't know how long it will take to be repaired."

As we were on a once-a-week flight, we began to think we might be in Ufa for a week. We had led training in Ufa four years before, but had not brought telephone numbers with us as we didn't expect to be there again this year. We asked for a telephone book, but there wasn't one. So there was no way to contact those we knew. Eventually we were offered a hotel room, with no soap and no toilet paper, and directed to where we could find a midday meal in the room with the pilots. It was one of the best meals we have ever had in Russia.

We were then offered a flight to Moscow, but that would have been almost as far from our destination as we were in Ufa! Fortunately fifty other passengers also refused this offer.

Much later on, we were told that Baby-flot Donaire was sending another plane from Rostov to collect us. Sadly, there was no way we could contact the unknown Ukrainian Christians, who were due to meet us in Rostov and then drive us the 6 hours to their home town, Toriez in Ukraine. However, as we walked through the arrivals gate at Rostov nine hours late, three peaceful smiling people were waiting for us, with no obvious signs that they had been waiting all day for many hours until 11.30pm.

Border crossing at 3am

At three o'clock in the morning we reached a border post, to be told they could only take Russians or Ukrainian's. So we must drive half an hour south to an international crossing point. As there were no other cars or lorries about, we thought we would be through this border post in no time. One of the three Ukranians, who had come to meet us, took our passports and visas into the office, which was out of sight. We waited and waited and waited!

About half an hour later he came back, rummaged in a bag in the car and returned to the border guard. Finally he joined us and told us the reason for the delay. Our visas were okay, but when the border guard looked at our passports, he said "These missionaries are very old, we must welcome them." This had started a conversation about God, and eventually the young man had come back to the car for a copy of Billy Graham's 'Peace with God' in Russian, which he then took back to the guard for him to read through the rest of the night. We eventually arrived at our destination at 5am with spring in the air. We went to bed and to sleep. When we woke at midday 3 feet of snow had landed in the 7 hours while we had slept.

'The Saints'

Our Christian host owned a repair garage, re-boring engines etc, next to the house. Because of the excellent work done there, it was where the police also brought their vehicles. It was nicknamed 'The Saints', by them too. The house and workshop had one tiny guard dog; a Chihuahua called Julia who was not allowed into the house in case she became too soft and failed to bark at strangers. She had a kennel outside, but had to watch the cats going in and out of the house as they pleased. Her efforts to negotiate the 3 feet of new snow were comical and very successful.

Staying with Galina in Nizhny Novgorod

We arrived for our first visit to Nizhny Novgorod, formerly the closed city named Gorky. There we found we were staying with Galina in her apartment, which consisted of a sitting room and two single bedrooms. She had moved out of hers onto the sitting room settee, so that we could each have a small room. Galina spoke no English and our Russian consisted of only a few basic phrases like 'hello' and 'how are you?' Galina was the hostess par excellence. She cooked meals for us and welcomed us as part of her family. She was living on her own but she had two sons living elsewhere and two grandchildren. We never did discover what had happened to her husband. Galina was a lot of fun and, as we had a dictionary with us, we somehow managed to communicate amid much laughter.

To take a shower was a real family affair. The bathroom was through the tiny kitchen, and the procedure for taking a shower was fairly complicated. First one had to announce the fact that you would like to take a shower. Next one undressed with the bathroom door closed. Then, standing in the empty bath behind the shower curtain, call out to Galina. She then turned on the kitchen hot tap so that the water pressure would reach the bathroom, but not too strongly. Next she came into the bathroom and adjusted the hot and cold taps without pulling aside the curtain one was hiding behind. Then it was time to take hold of the shower head, which was dangling rather precariously off its wall hook, as only one of its holder's three screws was still in the wall, and then pass it to her. Galina had somehow to test the temperature of the water coming through the shower head behind the curtain before one could proceed further. There was a definite sense of co-operation and achievement when one emerged clean and refreshed.

Galina's clothes were all in the same bedroom where I was, and you never knew when she might need them and come in to retrieve some of them. There was nowhere at all for me to put anything in the bedroom, so we somehow lived out of our suitcases. In David's room, which was no larger than mine, there was a hook behind the door and a small cupboard and a table where David could do his preparation.

David got quite a bad cough while we were there, and of course Galina heard him. So without a knock or a 'by your leave', Galina would appear in the middle of the night bringing in a bowl of steaming hot water and garlic to relieve his symptoms. What service.

One night a week Galina had a job and would be away, but she was replaced by a friend who came to look after us. We much enjoyed her too, and realised how important this was. We couldn't have answered the door or telephone, or known what to do in an emergency, or made ourselves understood to anyone who didn't know English. So they had certainly done the right thing in providing someone else to care for us.

A Communist's dilemma

After leading our second training course at the Pentecostal church in Nizhny Novgorod, built by its members, we celebrated together at a lunch given by the assistant pastor who had given up his medical career to help run this growing and successful church. We went to his home, where his wife had prepared a welcoming lunch for us all. We were unexpectedly joined by his mother, who was a retired English teacher. For once I didn't need an interpreter to talk to somebody. She had come to see these Englishmen, as she had never met a native English speaker before. All Russians had learnt from their fellow country-men, who in turn had learnt from those before them, there being no contact for the majority of Russians with any for-eigners during Soviet times. So she and I could sit beside each other on the sofa and talk together in English.

Her two sons had become Christians and also their wives, but not her or her husband. She told me she was glad that her sons had become Christians because they loved their wives and weren't drunkards or heavy smokers as so many were, but she had questions. For instance "Who made God?" I replied that I thought that if we knew who made God, we would be God. "Oh" she said, "you are a very wise woman." Telling our home church this story later, they burst into laughter and I got nicknamed "The wise woman of Winchester."

Novovyatsk

Another journey was to Kirov. We never travelled alone by train because we don't speak Russian. Train travel was much cheaper for Russians than for foreigners. So we'd pay for a young person to come with us, who had the time and who knew much more of the ropes than we did, and could interpret for us when needed.

This time we took the son of circus midgets with us. He had studied martial arts for his protection at school and college. He told us that the first thing he would think of when meeting a stranger was, 'How could I kill him?' But since he had become a Christian, his first thought was, 'How can I show him love?' He was great fun, and extremely fit and agile. He would swing himself up onto the top bunk in good monkey style.

On our arrival at Kirov a rather unsmiling Boris came to meet us, in black from head to foot. He led us to his red combi-van and we set off. He and our interpreter sat in front, and we were in the back. Soon the message came to us that we weren't going to Kirov, the city we were expecting to go to, but to a completely different city called Novovyatsk.

Boris apparently was pastor of the Baptist Church there, where we would each be leading the training course in a few days time. He took us to his ground floor flat and showed us the settee in their large sitting room, where we would sleep. It was an old house converted into flats, so the ground floor rooms were much larger than those built in Stalin's or Khrushchov's eras.

There were no cupboards of any sort, except for the glass fronted bookcase and drawers, which is usual in most Russian sitting rooms. We could put suitcases beside the bookcase, and that was our corner of life for the next two weeks.

Settling in

Left to ourselves, towards evening we began to get a little organised. We put on our most comfortable old clothes, made the settee into a bed and looked around to see where we could hang our few clothes. Eventually we noticed a tiny bracket between two pipes running down one wall that would take a hanger. So the problem was solved.

Our midget interpreter had to return home on the night train, so we were left with Boris and his wife and their three little girls, none of whom knew a word of English. Our next interpreter, Katya, could only arrive later the next day from Shadrinsk, an over-night train ride away.

Everything has to be drip dry, as you never see an iron. So in my luggage I have a small zip bag containing a makeshift clothesline, some clothes pegs and a tube of Travel Wash, which is concentrated detergent. When I opened the bag I found that the Travel Walsh had leaked and the clothesline and pegs with covered with it. Off I went to the bathroom to wash all this stuff off. There I found a small towel and folded them into it to dry off. I balanced this bundle on the arm of our bed-settee while I wondered what I could do with the contents to dry them off completely.

More surprises

Suddenly into this domestic scene came Boris with a plate of food in one hand, and with the other he deftly swept our bedding off the settee and put it on the floor in the corner. With it out flew the contents of the small towel, so clothes pegs clattered around the room. Boris was followed by his wife with more dishes and two couples, and some children who began to cycle round the room on their small bicycles. Our bed was turned back into a settee again and more chairs were found. When the dust settled so to speak, we discovered this was to be a feast in our honour, and the bishop and his wife had come to meet us. He happened to be Boris's elder brother. The other couple had come to interpret for us.

We felt rather sheepish meeting the bishop and his wife in our oldest comfortable clothes, but there we were sitting low down on the settee with our plates on the table about level with our mouths. It's not easy to eat beetroot soup from that position. But the food was delicious, the Bishop delightful and a good time of introduction was had by all. We seemed to be accepted.

The next day to our relief interpreter Katya arrived and was offered either a room in another building or she could sleep with the three young girls. None of us could contemplate her being in another building and the children were thrilled to have a captive grandmother in their room. So we all shook down in new surroundings. Boris himself came on our course, so he really knew how valuable his new leaders would be. As usual, we had 100% attendance in both groups, and after initial reticence everyone enjoyed it and gained immeasurably from it. Day by day, we got to know the family better and enjoyed each other to the full.

The course completed, we discovered that ice cream was the great love of the family. So to celebrate, we all went off, dressed to kill, to find the best ice cream parlour in town. By western standards you wouldn't have chosen it, but we found our table and celebrated to the full. By that time truths were emerging and Boris told us that when he had met us, if he hadn't liked the look of us he would have put us on the next train back to Nizhny, where we had come from! Fortunately he somehow did like the look of us, and here we were two weeks later thinking we had known each other for years. Yet again, we found it hard to tear ourselves away from such a lovely family and move on to our next city, Izhevsk.

Sasha Popov, an Izhevsk businessman, asked us to give training in Bible discussion group leading for the leaders in the student church he'd started. They meet on Sundays at 3pm so they can still also attend the traditional services of their mainstream churches. But here they learn responsibility and can discuss student issues.

Sasha is a great trainer of future leaders. He is now the Baptist Bishop of the Izhevsk Region, as well as continuing to earn his living as a businessman.

Another trainer of trainers

Katya came on to Izhevsk with us, this time not to interpret, but for the first time to train a group of students herself in Bible discussion leading. She had interpreted for us many times when we'd been leading it previously in other cities.

They loved her and she did so well. So instead of being limited to training twenty (two groups of ten) we trained thirty in this lively student church.

We had first met Katya in 1993 at a "Mission Volga" conference in Moscow. She was an experienced interpreter. She subsequently interpreted for us in many different cities in Russia, thinking nothing of travelling several days by train to join us.

Born during the war to a family of Old Believers, she was the 11th child and very sickly. The previous ten had all died. In the same week that the family cow died, her mother heard that he husband had been killed at The Front. Only Katya was left. She must be baptised as soon as possible.

In was April and the snow was too deep to get the Holy Bowl, so they decided to baptise her in the river. Three times they immersed the sickly child in the icy water, which was at its coldest as the ice was melting upstream. She was then placed on the shelf above the fire in the centre of the house to die.

Unexpectedly, she lives to tell the tale. Now in her 60s, she reckons the icy water gave her heart a kick start and she hasn't looked back.

Later she became a journalist working in one of Stalin's huge engineering plants. When she was invited to become a party member she felt she was totally unworthy because the Communist leaders were such good people. Eventually she was persuaded to become a party member and brought up her son as a Communist, which she later bitterly regretted. She once told us, "We thought our Communist leaders were heroes, but now we know they were monsters."

By the time we met her she had become a Christian and had started a Baptist church in her home town of Shadrinsk. The next time we met, she told us her son had become a Christian too. How she rejoiced. Through the years we have had many shared experiences travelling and working together.

One day we were sharing about each other and mentioned our ages, and I remember saying, "Katya, you could be my daughter." She is a prodigious letter writer and still keeps in touch with us, always starting her letters "Dear Mom and Dad." She is a fun loving dauchka.

Some truths to live by

Just as a car isn't initially sold without a manual, or a piece of machinery without an instruction book, so God hasn't left me without a manual to live by. In my school days when I was studying to pass exams about the Bible, I never realised it was also a book to live by. Here is some of its every-day wisdom and instruction that I find particularly helpful.

> *All Scripture is inspired by God and is profitable for teaching, for reproof, for correction, and for training in righteousness, that the man of God may be complete, equipped for every good work.* 2 Timothy 3:16-17

The writers of the Bible have been inspired by God the Holy Spirit, and it is for:

> Teaching us the facts.
> Telling us where we go wrong.
> Getting us back on track.
> Training us in how to live rightly.

So that I may be a complete person and equipped for all the good things that God wants me to do.

> *Like newborn babes, long for the pure spiritual milk, that by it you may grow up to salvation....* 1 Peter 2:2

Just as a baby needs milk, so do I need God's Word to grow up. As a Christian I can't do without God's Word. I need to read it, study it, memorised it and act upon it. I need it, whether I feel like it or not; just as we eat in order to live, whether we feel like it or not.

> *For by grace you have been saved through faith; and this is not your own doing, it is the gift of God - not because of works, lest any man should boast.* Ephesians 2:8-9.

This statement gives me tremendous assurance and freedom. Even the trust I have put in Jesus Christ is a gift. I don't deserve his saving grace, nor can I earn it. I don't need to try to be somebody or strive to do special things. I am free to be myself. Jesus paying my debt has freed me.

> *For we are his workmanship, created in Christ Jesus for good works, which God prepared beforehand, that we should walk in them.* Ephesians 2:10.

Here I learn that God is the master carpenter. Someone may be a piece of soft pine, I may be more like a piece of ebony, but God as a craftsman is fashioning me into what he wants me to be. Also he has already planned the good things he wants me to do. So I can wake up in the morning, even with a headache, and know I don't have to make myself into a good Christian. He is working in me and I know he has a plan for me that day that he has already prepared with these encouragements. I can step out of bed into the new day with expectation.

> *Then the Lord God said, "It is not good that the man should be alone; I will make him a helper fit for him."* Genesis 2:18.

As I keep this purpose as my number one aim, it clarifies all sorts of questions as to what my priorities should be. David needs the particular help that I can give him and I can be fulfilled in giving it.

If he needs to talk something through with me or needs my help to know what to wear or many other things, I am being his suitable helper and fulfilling my purpose and being fulfilled in the doing of it. I can respect his need to need me. He is not stupid if he is unsure what goes with what of his clothing.

> *Be subject to one another out of reverence for Christ.....*
> *As the church is subject to Christ, so let wives also be*
> *subject in everything to their husbands. Husbands,*
> *love your wives, as Christ loved the church and gave*
> *himself up for her..... "For this reason a man shall*
> *leave his father and mother and be joined to his wife,*
> *and the two shall become one." This is a great mystery,*
> *and I take it to mean Christ and the church; however,*
> *let each one of you love his wife as himself, and let the*
> *wife see that she respects her husband.* Ephesians 5:21-33.

This tells of the visual aid that Christian marriage is to the world, depicting the relationship between Christ and his church. The husband loving his wife and his wife responding by putting him first and fitting into his life. What a privilege to be part of God's purpose in this visual aid by playing my right role, and what an incentive to do it and to go on doing it.

> *Have no anxiety about anything, but in everything by*
> *prayer and supplication with thanksgiving let your re-*
> *quests be made known to God. And the peace of God,*
> *which passes all understanding, will keep your hearts*
> *and your minds in Christ Jesus.* Philippians 4:6-7.

It is a well known fact that worry can seriously affect your health. I used to be a tremendous worrier before I found Jesus. I was always tired and catching colds etc. Here we are told very emphatically not to worry, but to swap it for prayer, 'making our requests known to God'. Someone has said, to emphasise the point, "Why pray when you can worry?" When we pray instead of worrying, the outcome will be peace beyond our understanding, which will keep our hearts and minds firmly in Christ Jesus. We can have peace in the midst of the most difficult circumstances.

> *Therefore do not be anxious, saying, "What shall we eat?" or "What shall we drink?" or "What shall we wear?"...... your heavenly Father knows that you need them all. But seek first his kingdom and his righteousness, and all these things shall be yours as well. Therefore do not be anxious about tomorrow for tomorrow will be anxious for itself. Let the days own trouble be sufficient for the day.* Matthew 6:31-34.

So many people carry heavy burdens because they're worrying about the future. When I had cancer in 1984, I really learnt how to live by this teaching of Jesus; first and only be concerned for today's concerns. I found I couldn't live with the "what ifs?" What if I get cancer again? As Paul writes in 2 Corinthians 10:5, I had to take every thought of worrying about tomorrow into captivity to obey Christ.

It was worth having cancer to learn to live without worry, whatever the difficulty or problem.

> *Count it all joy, my brethren, when you meet various trials, for you know that the testing of your faith produces steadfastness. And let steadfastness have its full effect, that you may be perfect and complete, lacking in nothing.* James 1:2-4.

Being Christians doesn't exempt us from facing trials. In the West we have such an easy life compared to most of the rest of the world. Our trials hardly begin to compare with theirs. There is almost the feeling around that we deserve a life without any problems at all, so when trials do come we are shocked and indignant, and sometimes even angry.

James sees that trials will work patience in us and the outcome of patience is that we will be perfect, complete and lacking nothing. What prizes result from patience? Could we want more? That's why he says, "When trials come, be joyful because of their outcome." What a different attitude this is to the self-pity that trials can so easily evoke.

> *If any of you lacks wisdom, let him ask God, who gives to all men generously and without reproaching, and it will be given him. But let him ask in faith, with no doubting...... For that person must not suppose that the double-minded man, unstable in all his ways, will receive anything from the Lord.* James 1:5-8.

Wisdom is something I need often every day. Here we are told to ask for it, but on the condition that we ask in faith, not doubting. Then he will give it. But if I'm half trusting and half not, I am double-minded then it's no good expecting to get wisdom. I am an unstable person.

> *We know that in everything God works for good with those who love him, who are called according to his purpose.*   Romans 8:28.

This is God's promise. However bad we think an experience is, we can be sure this is what God will do. We do not have children, but we look back and see what we have been able to do and be involved in, much of which wouldn't have been possible if we'd had children. In the Stewards' Trust, not having teenagers growing up beside us didn't give away the fact that our ages were becoming nearer their parents than theirs. So we could more easily come alongside them as friends, which we did.

Having cancer turned into such a blessing because of what I learned through it enabling me to identify with others.

David being made redundant by Intercon was hard at the time, but we look back with thankfulness. Otherwise we would never have started The 2 Tim 2 Trust, which enabled us to continue Purpose Holidays and offer training courses in many parts of the world.

Romans 8:28 is a promise, so one first has to believe it, then experience it and then expect it. Expecting good to come out of every questionable experience, trauma, illness or whatever, takes the sting out of it, and makes it far easier to handle.

> *And what you have heard from me before many witnesses entrust to faithful men who will be able to teach others also.*   2 Timothy 2:2.

While we were thinking of a name for the trust that we were setting up to work for, we sat up in bed one morning and said, "What about The 2 Tim 2 Trust?" And that's what it became. David's training with The Navigators in the States, which has steered so much of his Christian thinking since, put great emphasis into building into people's lives that they may grow to teach others also, and in this way multiply. So my second priority is to be in constant touch with some, to try to build into their lives so that they may be able to teach others also. What wonderful friends of all ages I have through this priority, and what a joy it is to watch them grow.

> **So what ever you wish that men would do to you, do so to them.** Matthew 7:12.

Always a big question in our daily lives is, how should I react to people, how should I help people, how should I treat people in different circumstances? This piece of advice simplifies what to do and sometimes leads to surprising answers. It also changes as we grow in life, and the ways we like to be treated change too.

How would I want to be treated when I'm tired after a journey? Treat someone else in the same way. Suppose I'm feeling lonely or left out? Treat someone else in the same way. How would I like it if someone arrived unexpectedly, whom I hadn't seen for ages, even though it was very inconvenient? Treat someone else in the same.

What about, if someone is feeling low and just wants to talk to me, or be with me for a short while? I would want them to come at any hour, convenient or not. So if I feel low I should go to them, whether I think it might be convenient for them or not.

> *For here we have no lasting city, but we seek the city which is to come.* Hebrews 13:14.

God's kingdom is a different kind of kingdom from those in the world, though within it. So I shouldn't be surprised to increasingly feel that I don't belong to the kingdom of this world.

> *Whatever your task, work heartily, as serving the Lord and not men, knowing that from the Lord you will receive the iheritance as your reward, you are serving the Lord Christ.* Colossians 3:23-24.

I find that if I apply this directive it changes my attitude to the task that I'm engaged in, because my motive for doing it is different.

Am I working for a boss? Yes, but above that I'm working for the Lord.

Am I making a bed? Yes, but I'm doing it for Jesus.

Am I offering tea to a difficult person? Yes, I'm serving the Lord Christ.

> *So we are ambassadors for Christ ...* 2 Corinthians 5:20.

We live in a foreign country representing our King, and making known his message to that country. We don't belong to that country or its customs because we belong to another kingdom. It's not surprising that we feel we don't belong here.

> *... as they were looking on, he was lifted up, and a cloud took him out of their sight. And while they were gazing into heaven as he went, behold two men stood by them in white robes, and said, "Men of Galilee, why do you stand looking into heaven? This Jesus, who was taken up from you into heaven, will come in the same way as you saw him go into heaven."* Acts 1:9-11.

One of the greatest truths to live by is that Jesus is one day going to return to this world, not as Saviour this time but as Lord and King and Judge.

There are just four references in the Bible to the Lord's Supper or Holy Communion, and Christians all over the world gather to share this symbolic meal to remember his death for the payment of our sins.

By contrast there are over 300 references in the Bible to his return to this earth, when he will take his rightful place as Lord of the whole world. We eagerly look forward to his coming. We wait expectantly for his return. What an event to look forward to!

These are some of my Truths to Live By, but I must also remember, as the truth inscribed in my wedding ring says. *Unless the Lord builds the house, those who build it labour in vain.* Psalm 127:1

Three helpful tortoises

 We have three friends who are tortoises. They are called Facts, Faith and Feelings.

Feelings　　　　**Faith**　　　　**Facts**

They are walking one behind the other along the top of a wall.

If Faith follows Facts, Feelings follow.

But if Faith follows Feelings, they all fall off.

Autumn

Today is a beautiful day at the beginning of September in 2008. There is just a touch and a feel of autumn in the air. Our caravan sits in the drive looking a little as if it wouldn't quite like another trip around Europe on Purpose Holidays. It has been such a friend and base for many adventures, and a welcome home for others as well as for us.

It's not quite a classic that old Rovers or Jaguars are looking to partner. But neither would today's caravaners appreciate its simplicity and lack of a fridge and a shower. A caravan expert said that its only purpose now would be as an office on a building site. We would never allow such an indignity. So it has its royal position on the drive fulfilling several helpful roles, like an extra spare room and a store for garden games. Last year it took on the role of storing apples until the mice discovered the haul and had a ball.

Perhaps one day a discerning caravan lover will discover its uniqueness, and rejuvenate and care for it as it should be cared for. Until that day it stays with all its store of memories, which cover a full 25 years of our lives.

In March 2007 we were co-ordinating a seminar in St Petersburg on "Christians at Work" and re-met Volodia Tcherkasskih and his family. He was coordinator of 'Mission Volga', which was our first introduction to Russia in 1992. And through that mission we became acquainted with many pastors in many cities. These and others requested David's courses, which we were able to lead in 18 Russian cities and 2 in Ukraine. Several years ago Volodia said to me, "Shirley you'll be good for Russia until you're 80." In March, I reminded him of this, but also said, "Volodia, this summer we've got a problem, I'm going to be 80." Quick as lightning came back the reply, "In that case we will have to have an extension till you're 90." Volodia's optimism is touching, but life in Russian cities outside Moscow and St Petersburg is fairly spartan. Our hearts may be willing, but our bodies may not cope in just the same way as a few years ago. After all it is the autumn of our lives.

Last summer was my 80th birthday and I was feted like a queen with so much attention. It was enough to turn one's head. Our lives must be slower now, but I can still live by the truths I have learnt from God's Word over the last 50 years.

I hope you've enjoyed rambling through my life with me. Perhaps we've both found some nuggets to remind us of *apples of gold in a setting of silver*, that quickens our step and hums a tune in our head as we follow the path that leads us into tomorrow -

Index